DESCARTES

STUDIES IN PHILOSOPHY

CONSULTING EDITOR:

V. C. CHAPPELL,

The University of Chicago

A Random House Study in the History of Philosophy

DESCARTES

A STUDY OF HIS PHILOSOPHY

ANTHONY KENNY

Balliol College, Oxford University

RANDOM HOUSE   New York

579864

Manufactured in the United States of America
Design by Diana Hrisinko

PREFACE

Descartes advised readers of his *Principles of Philosophy* to read the book first as they would a novel, without stopping; and then to read it a second time more slowly, marking with a pen places where they found difficulty. "If the book is taken up a third time," he predicted confidently, "the reader will discover the solution of the greater part of the difficulties which have formerly been marked."

This book is designed to help undergraduate and graduate students in understanding Descartes' philosophy, but is not meant to be used as a substitute for the reading of his own works. Rather, it is directed to those who have read them twice in the manner prescribed above, but who find that the penciled queries do not

entirely disappear upon third reading. It is devoted principally to the topics discussed in the *Meditations*, treating epistemology, metaphysics, and philosophy of mind
rather than methodology, ethics, or philosophy of science.

References to Descartes' own works are made within
the text in parentheses by means of the following ab-
breviations. AT: *Oeuvres de Descartes*, Charles Adam
and Paul Tannery, editors (Paris: Cerf, 1897 and 1913),
13 volumes; HR: *The Philosophical Works of Descartes*,
Elizabeth S. Haldane and G. R. T. Ross, translators
(Cambridge: Cambridge University Press, 1911, 1931),
2 volumes, paperback, 1967. References to works of
other writers are given in notes collected at the end of
the book.

Part of the material of Chapters Four and Five
overlaps with my paper "Cartesian Privacy," in George
Pitcher's collection of critical essays on Wittgenstein,
Modern Studies in Philosophy (New York: Doubleday,
1966). I am grateful for permission to quote from the
following translations, which I have used eclectically:
Descartes: Philosophical Writings. A selection translated and edited by Elizabeth Anscombe and Peter
Thomas Geach (London: Nelson, 1954). *The Philosophical Works of Descartes*, rendered into English by
Elizabeth S. Haldane and G. R. T. Ross (Copyright,
1931 by Cambridge University Press, London).

Drafts of particular chapters of this book were read
to colloquia or seminars at several universities in Great
Britain and the United States. Much of the material in
the book was used in my course at the University of
Chicago in the Fall term of 1966; I am indebted to those

who took part in these discussions and lectures for their helpful criticisms. In particular, I am grateful to Willis Doney, Harry Frankfurt, Elizabeth Anscombe, Vere Chappell, and Ralph Walker for their valuable suggestions.

A. K.

CONTENTS

DESCARTES

ONE

LIFE AND WORKS

René Descartes was thirty-two years younger than Shakespeare and forty-six years older than Newton. He was born in 1596 in the village in Touraine that is now called La Haye-Descartes. His mother died when he was a year old, leaving him "a dry cough and a pale complexion." He was a sickly child, expected to die young. When he went to school he was dispensed from early morning exercises and awarded a private room, where he acquired a lifelong habit of meditating in bed. From his eleventh to his nineteenth year he studied classics and philosophy at the newly founded Jesuit college of La Flèche. He always recalled with respect the talents and devotion of his teachers, but he regarded their scholastic doctrines at first with suspicion and later with contempt. Among all his lessons, only mathematics really delighted him "on account of the certainty and clarity of its reasoning."

In 1616, having taken a degree in law at Poitiers, Descartes abandoned his studies in favor of "the great book of the world." At the age of twenty-two he enrolled as an unpaid volunteer in the army of the Dutch Prince Maurice of Orange. While in Holland he discussed mathematics, physics, and logic with the savant Isaac Beeckman, for whom he wrote a brief treatise on music. In 1619 he transferred to the army of the Duke of Bavaria, who was warring against the Elector Frederick, son-in-law of King James I.

During this winter Descartes acquired a conviction of his task as a philosopher. He spent November 10, 1619, beside a stove, engrossed in the meditations that he records in the second part of the *Discourse on Method*. He conceived the idea of undertaking, single-handed, a reform of human learning that would display all disciplines as branches of a single wonderful science. When he went to sleep, full of ardor for his project, he had three dreams that he regarded as prophetic signs of divine vocation.

Soon afterward he left the army, but several years passed before he settled permanently to philosophical studies. From 1620 to 1625 he traveled in Germany, Holland, and Italy, returning to France for a period in 1622 to settle his property in such a way as to free him forever from the necessity of earning a living. From 1625 to 1627 he lived the life of a gentleman in Paris, mixing in society, gambling, becoming involved in a duel over a love affair. The fragmentary writings that survive from this period show that he worked on mechanical and mathematical puzzles and continued to harbor great secret ambitions. In 1627 he intervened impressively in the discussion of a lecture before the Papal Nuncio and was exhorted by Cardinal Berulle, the founder of the French Oratory, to devote himself to the reform of philosophy.

It was probably at this time that Descartes began to write his *Rules for the Direction of the Mind*. This never-completed Latin work, first published in 1701, shows that the universal science of which Descartes dreamed was to be achieved by the application of mathematical techniques to every sphere of knowledge.

In 1628 Descartes left for Holland, where he lived until 1649. He chose the country because he liked the climate and he hoped to be free from the distractions of the city and in particular from the danger of early morning callers. He continued to practice as a Catholic amid Protestant surroundings. During these twenty years, he lived in thirteen different houses and kept his address carefully secret from all but his closest friends.

Later generations may be grateful for Descartes' passion for solitude. Because of it, most of his philosophical discussion with his contemporaries was conducted by letter. His correspondence forms a very substantial part of his corpus of philosophical writings. His chief correspondent was the Franciscan friar Marin Mersenne, a senior school contemporary who had worked with him on optics during his Paris period. Courteous and erudite, Mersenne shared all Descartes' interests and wrote him regular letters packed with scientific and philosophical queries on every topic from transubstantiation to chimney cleaning. He acted as Descartes' literary agent, handling the publication of his works, forwarding his correspondence to thinkers throughout Europe, and keeping him informed of recent scientific discoveries. Among Descartes' other correspondents at this time were Père Gibieuf, a priest of Berulle's Oratory, and Constantijn Huygens, the father of the more famous Christian Huygens.

Descartes lived in Holland comfortably but not luxuriously. He devoted one day a week to correspondence. He read little. In twenty years, he said, he did not open a scholastic textbook. He had little respect for the classics; there was no more need to know Latin and Greek, he thought, than the rustic dialects of Brittany. He brought few books from Paris; among them were a Bible and a *Summa* of Saint Thomas. He experimented in optics and physiology, grinding his own lenses and purchasing carcasses from the butcher for dissection. When a stranger asked to see his library, he pointed to a half-dissected calf: "There are my books," he said. Descartes trusted experiment rather than learning, but more than either he trusted his own philosophical reflection. Even so, he did not devote great time to meditation. His policy, he said, was "never to spend beyond a very few hours daily in thoughts which occupy the imagination, and a very few hours yearly in those which occupy the understanding, and to give all the remaining time to the relaxation of the senses and the repose of mind."

In Holland Descartes did not live entirely without company. He sometimes visited neighboring universities and would entertain members of their faculties who were attracted by his ideas, such as Henri Reneri and Henri Regius of the University of Utrecht. In 1635 he had an illegitimate daughter, whom he christened Francine. Her death at the age of five caused him great grief.

His work during his first years in Holland was predominantly mathematical and physical. He laid the foundations of analytical geometry; he worked on refraction and propounded the law of sines. By 1632 Descartes had in hand an ambitious work entitled "The World," in which he sought to explain "the nature of light, the sun and the fixed stars which emit it; the heavens which transmit it; the planets, the comets, and the earth which reflect it; all the terrestrial bodies which are either colored or transparent or luminous; and Man its spectator." In this work he jettisoned the Aristotelian notions of substantial form and natural movements, and sought to explain physics and physiology in terms of the purely geometrical properties and spatial motions of matter.

This treatise was ready for the press when Descartes learned of the condemnation of Galileo by the Inquisition. The decree forbade it to be taught, "even as a hypothesis," that the earth moved around the sun. This was just what Descartes had done. Anxious to avoid any dispute with the ecclesiastical authorities, he returned the treatise to his desk. Some fragments of it were published after his death, and much of its material was incorporated in the *Principles of Philosophy*, but it was neither published nor preserved as a whole.

In 1637, however, Descartes decided to make public "some specimens of his method." He published anonymously his *Dioptric*, his *Meteors*, and his *Geometry*, introducing them with a "discourse on the right way to use one's reason and seek truth in the sciences." The work was written in French; even women, he said, might understand it. The *Discourse on Method* was destined to become immensely more famous than the works to which it was a preface; initially it caused much less sensation than the *Dioptric* and the *Geometry*, which brought their author into collision with the foremost mathematicians of his day, such as Pierre de Fermat and Gilles Personne de Roberval. The controversy was fierce: throughout his life Descartes found it difficult to remain polite in the face of contradiction.

While working on his scientific treatises, Descartes had become more and more interested in questions of epistemology and metaphysics. "The whole of philosophy," he wrote later, "is like a tree, whose roots are metaphysics, whose trunk is physics, and whose branches are all the other sciences, which can be reduced to three principal ones, namely medicine, mechanics, and morals." Descartes' interest in the metaphysical foundations of physics is shown already in the correspondence with Mersenne in 1630, in which he insists that the eternal truths of logic and mathematics were freely created by God. The fourth part of the *Discourse* contains, in a marvelously brief and lucid summary, most of the main items of Descartes' metaphysics: the universal doubt, the *cogito*, the arguments for the distinction between soul and body and for the existence of God, the identification of the essence of soul with thought and of the essence of body with extension. But it was not until 1640 that Descartes completed his fullest statement of his system: the *Metaphysical Meditations*, which combined literary beauty and philosophical genius in a manner unsurpassed since Plato.

Before publication the *Meditations* were sent to Mersenne to be communicated for discussion to a number of scholars and thinkers. After the manuscript had circulated, six sets of objections were received; they were printed, with Descartes' replies, in a long appendix to the first edition of the work, in 1641.

The first objections, submitted by the scholastic Caterus, archpriest of Alkmaar, concerned principally the ontological argument for the existence of God. The second objections were attributed by Mersenne to "a group of philosophers and theologians" and were probably written in part by himself. They were respectful in tone and drew from Descartes some glosses on the *cogito*, a statement of his distinction between analytic and synthetic method, and an axiomatic presentation of his arguments *more geometrico*.

The third objections were written by Thomas Hobbes, eight years Descartes' senior and temporarily exiled in Paris. This contact between the two greatest philosophers of the age was not cordial. "Mr. Hobbes was wont to say," wrote Aubrey, "that had Des Cartes kept himself wholy to Geometrie that he had been the best Geometer in the world but that his head did not lye for Philosophy." Hobbes' objections were often blunt, and Descartes' replies often terse. Hobbes criticized from the point of a nominalist materialist; in reply Descartes was forced to clarify his position on the relation between ideas and mental images.

The author of the fourth objections, the acute Augustinian theologian Antoine Arnauld, had studied the text of the *Meditations* more closely than the other critics. He raised the question of whether Descartes was not arguing in a circle in appealing to clear and distinct ideas to prove the existence of God while appealing to the veracity of God to guarantee clear and distinct ideas. He also canvassed the difficulties that Descartes' theories raised for the Catholic doctrine of transubstantiation. Later, however, Arnauld became a convinced Cartesian and incorporated some of Descartes' ideas in his *Port Royal Logic*.

In the fifth objections the priest-philosopher Pierre Gassendi, like Descartes an enemy of Aristotelianism, made a searching criticism of Cartesian dualism. (He addressed Descartes with ironic respect as "O mind!" and was in turn nicknamed "O flesh!") The controversy lasted beyond a single book, into Gassendi's *Instantiae* and Descartes' Letter to Clerselier. After attack and counterattack, instance and counterinstance, the two philosophers were reconciled in 1647.

The 1641 edition of the *Meditations* concludes with a sixth set of objections and answers, which add little to the other five sets. Criticisms continued to come in after publication. One set of objections from the voluble and facetious Jesuit Pierre Bourdin drew from Descartes an unnecessarily long and occasionally witty set of annotations, which were printed in the second edition of the *Meditations*, along with a letter to Father Dinet, Bourdin's Jesuit superior. Of more value, but not reprinted, were the criticisms of an anonymous geometer, to which Descartes replied in August, 1641, in the Letter to Hyperaspistes.

Critical reaction to the *Meditations* was not only

literary. Descartes was denounced to the magistrates by Gisbert Voetius, the rector of Utrecht, as a dangerous propagator of atheism, and for a time it looked as if he was in danger of being arrested and having his books burned. Later, at the University of Leyden, he was accused of the heresy of Pelagianism, and had to call upon influential friends to intervene to ensure his safety. There are extant the tracts that he wrote in defense of his orthodoxy: one to Voetius and one to the trustees of the University of Leyden.

Descartes' most enthusiastic supporter at Utrecht had been Regius, the professor of botany and medicine, whose aggressive publicizing of his views had led to the controversy with Voetius. But master and disciple soon quarreled, and in 1647 Descartes wrote a tract against Regius, known as the "Notes on a Programme," which contains useful clarifications of his doctrine of innate ideas.

During these years of controversy Descartes gained a new friend: the exiled Princess Elizabeth, daughter of the Elector Frederick, against whom Descartes had once soldiered. He corresponded with her from 1643 until his death, answering her acute questions about his writings, favoring her with a wealth of medical and moral advice, and consoling her on the execution of her uncle King Charles I. In 1646 he dedicated to her his third major work, *The Principles of Philosophy*. This was written in short paragraphs as a school textbook in the optimistic expectation that it would replace the scholastic manuals. Its first part sketches briskly the metaphysics of the *Meditations*, and its second, third, and fourth parts deal with the principles of physical science, especially the laws of motion, the theory of vortices, and the explanation of astronomical phenomena and the nature of weight, heat, and light. Descartes' account of the solar system is disguisedly heliocentric and discreetly evolutionary. He was careful to explain that he was describing not how the world in fact was made, but how God might have made it if he had pleased otherwise.

In 1648 Descartes was visited at Egmond by a twenty-year-old admirer named Francis Burman. He entertained the young man at dinner and gave full and lively answers to his queries about points in the *Meditations*, *Principles*, and *Discourse*. Burman's notes of this interview are extant and provide a vivid picture of the philosopher's table talk. Later in the same year Father Mersenne died; his place as Descartes' chief correspondent was taken by Claude Clerselier.

Descartes' correspondence with Princess Elizabeth led him to reflect further on the relationship between the body and the soul and to construct an ethical system of Stoic flavor. He developed these reflections into a treatise entitled *The Passions of the Soul*, which was published in 1649.

By this time Descartes had acquired another royal patron. Clerselier's brother-in-law, Pierre Chanut, was ambassador to Queen Christina of Sweden, then in her early twenties. Through Chanut, Descartes had corresponded with Queen Christina about love and about the supreme good; he had sent her a copy of *The Passions of the Soul*. The queen was so favorably impressed that she invited Descartes to her court, sending an admiral with a warship to transport him to Sweden. After some hesitation, Descartes agreed to sacrifice his solitude and left for Stockholm in September, 1649. The move was disastrous. He felt lonely and out of place; he was employed in writing a ballet and was forced to rise at five o'clock to instruct the queen in philosophy. Once he had hoped by his medical studies to discover the secret of prolonging life. Now he fell a victim to the rigors of the Swedish winter. While nursing a sick friend, he caught pneumonia and died on February 11, 1650. He was buried in Sweden, but later his body was transported to France where it now rests in the church of Saint Germain des Près. His skull is exhibited in the Musée de L'Homme in the Palais de Chaillot in Paris.

Many unpublished pieces were found among his papers at Stockholm. The most important was the *Rules for the Direction of the Mind,* already mentioned. Others included the *Treatise on Man* (published by Clerselier in 1664) and an unfinished French dialogue entitled *The Search After Truth,* which first appeared in a Latin translation in 1701. This dialogue is useful for the light it casts on Descartes' method of doubt and on the nature of the *cogito.* The discussion is divided between three characters: Epistemon (who represents scholastic philosophy), Polyander (the common man), and Eudoxus (the mouthpiece of Descartes himself). Like the interview described in Burman's notes, these posthumous papers illuminate and complement the better-known works of Descartes, which were published during his lifetime.

TWO

CARTESIAN DOUBT

Once in his lifetime, Descartes said, a man who seeks truth must call in doubt whatever can be doubted. Many of our beliefs were acquired in childhood before we attained the use of reason. They derive from un-critical sense perception, unreasoning instinct, and the testimony of unreliable educators. Our minds are like a canvas botched by apprentice painters; our beliefs con-stitute a shaky edifice on rotten foundations. The can-vas must be wiped clean if reason is to paint upon it; the house of belief must be pulled up and rebuilt from the foundations. We must doubt everything about which there can be the slightest uncertainty. We can-not, of course, test each belief in turn to see whether it admits of doubt; but we can examine the foundations on which our beliefs in general depend. This is what Descartes set himself to do in his *First Meditation* (AT VII, 17–23; HR I, 144; cf. also the *Discourse*, AT VI, 32; HR I, 101; *Principles*, AT VIII, 5–6; HR I, 219–221; *The Search After Truth*, AT X, 509 ff.; HR I, 313 ff.).

The most apparently solid of our beliefs derive from the senses; even the testimony of others comes to us through hearing. The existence of perceptible objects seems more assured than that of God or the soul. Yet the senses sometimes deceive us, and it is imprudent to trust where one has once been deceived.

But, Descartes objects to himself,

> . . . although the senses may sometimes deceive us about some minute or remote objects, yet there are many other facts as to which doubt is plainly impossible, although these are gathered from the same source: e.g. that I am here, sitting by the fire, wearing a winter cloak, holding this paper in my hands, and so on. Again, these hands and my whole body— how can their existence be denied? (AT VII, 18; HR I, 145)

But madmen sometimes have the delusion that their bodies are made of glass, or think themselves to be pumpkins. What reason has Descartes to think that his senses are more trustworthy than theirs? But there is no need for him to suppose himself mad; it is enough to recall that he sometimes has dreams as wild as the delusions of the insane. Certainly he has often dreamed that he was sitting cloaked by the fire when he was really undressed in bed. It is no good telling himself that now at least he is awake; does he not remember having been formerly deceived by just such reflections when asleep? There is no criterion by which one can certainly distinguish sleep from the waking state; how then can anyone be certain that his whole life is not a dream and that everything the senses teach him is not false?

But surely even dreams are made up of elements drawn from reality.

> Suppose I am dreaming, and these particulars, that I open my eyes, shake my head, put out my hand, are incorrect; suppose even that I have no such hand, no such body; at any rate it has to be admitted that the things that appear in sleep are like painted representations, which cannot have been formed except in the likeness of real objects. So at least these general kinds of things, eyes, head, hands, body must not be imaginary but real objects. (AT VII, 20; HR I, 146)

Perhaps these bodies, in turn, are not real elements, but are fictional composites comparable to the creations of a painter. But then the simpler elements out of which these bodies are composed—corporeal nature in general, extension, shape, size, number, place, and time—must surely themselves be real.

The pursuit thus far of the method of doubt would lead to the conclusion that the natural sciences are doubtful, while the mathematical sciences have an element of indubitable certainty. For physics, astronomy, and medicine deal with composite objects, while arithmetic and geometry treat of very simple and very general objects without worrying whether these objects exist in nature or not. "Whether I am awake or asleep, two and three add up to five, and a square has only four sides; and it seems impossible for such obvious truths to fall under a suspicion of being false."

Even mathematics, however, is not immune to Cartesian doubt.

> One reason is that people have made mistakes in reasoning in such matters, and have held as certain and self-evident what we see to be false. A more important reason is that we have been told that God who created us can do all that he desires, and we do not yet know whether he may not have willed to create us in such a way that we shall always be deceived even in the things that we think ourselves to know best. (*Principles*, AT VIII, 6; HR I, 220)

Perhaps there are no extended bodies, no shape or size or place, and perhaps it is just that God makes it appear to us that there are. Perhaps He makes us go wrong whenever we add two and three, or count the sides of a square. Some people, of course, are prepared to deny the existence of an omnipotent creator. No matter. The less power is attributed to the source of our being, the more likely are we to be so imperfect as to be always in error.

Descartes concludes from all this that none of his previous beliefs is immune from well-founded doubt; if he seeks certainty, he must refrain from assent to any of them. This is possible, because "we experience a freedom within ourselves which enables us to abstain from giving our assent to things of which we have no certain knowledge" (*Principles*, AT VIII, 6; HR I, 221). It is not, indeed, likely that our beliefs are all false: "they are doubtful in a way, as has been shown, but are yet highly probable, and far more reasonably believed than denied." But habit presses us to believe them implicitly; to avoid this pressure it is necessary to go to the opposite extreme and pretend that they are all false.

I will suppose, then, not that there is a supremely good God, the source of truth; but that there is an evil spirit, who is supremely powerful and intelligent, and does his utmost to deceive me. I will suppose that sky, air, earth, colours, shapes, sounds and all external objects are mere delusive dreams, by means of which he lays snares for my credulity. I will consider myself as having no hands, no eyes, no flesh, no blood, no senses, but just having a false belief that I have all these things. I will remain firmly fixed in this meditation, and resolutely take care that, so far as in me lies, even if it is not in my power to know some truth, I may not assent to falsehood nor let myself be imposed upon by that deceiver, however powerful and intelligent he may be. (AT VII, 23; HR I, 148)

Descartes' style is hypnotic. We must go back over the argument to see how far it should carry conviction. Few would quarrel with the starting point: it is true that we grow up uncritically accepting many beliefs which may be false. But is it necessary, in order to rectify this, that we should on some one occasion call in question all our beliefs? Can we not correct them piecemeal? Descartes gives "a homely example" to explain the rationale of his universal doubt. Suppose, he says, that a man

. . . had a basket of apples, and fearing that some of them were rotten, wanted to take those out lest they might make the rest go bad, how could he do that? Would he not first turn the whole of the apples out of the basket, and look them over one by one, and then having selected those which he saw not to be rotten, place them again in the basket and leave

out the others? (*Seventh Objections*, AT VII, 481;
HR II, 282)

But why do I have to take out all the apples at once
(i.e., reject all my beliefs)? Why can't I take the apples
out singly and inspect them one by one (i.e., critically
examine each belief in turn)? Descartes' answer is that
leaving the bad apples in the basket will corrupt the
good ones. But my retaining false beliefs cannot make
my true beliefs less true. No, says Descartes, but it makes
them less certain: we must "separate the false from the
true lest the presence of the former should produce a
general uncertainty about all." But why should the fact
that I have *some* false beliefs prevent my being certain
about *any*? Can *none* of my beliefs be certain unless
all are certain? Descartes' argument presupposes this,
but he offers no proof of it.

In fact, Descartes believed that all human sciences
formed a unified whole, so linked together that it could
be held in one's mind with no more difficulty than the
series of natural numbers (AT X, 215, 361). If this is so,
then a man's scientific beliefs must either be all true or
all doubtful. But this is not a premise to which Descartes can fairly appeal in order to convince the uncom-
mitted reader of the need of the method of universal
doubt. Instead, he uses metaphors—such as that of the
house with unsound foundations—that suggest that a
man's beliefs are a system that holds up or collapses as
a whole (*Seventh Objections*, AT VII, 531; HR II,
325).

Answering metaphor with metaphor, an objector
might say that when we attempt to criticize and correct

our beliefs we are in the position of a man trying to repair a leaky boat on the high seas. It is not possible to take the boat altogether to pieces and rebuild it afresh: the rotting timbers have to be replaced one by one. Without metaphor, we may say that it is impossible to criticize and correct a belief except in the light of other beliefs, and it follows that it is impossible to criticize the totality of one's beliefs at a single time.

 A universal doubt is neither necessary nor rational; and Descartes' own execution of his plan falls far short of "doubting whatever can be doubted." If he believed that the senses have sometimes deceived him and that mathematicians have made mistakes, then it seems that he must be trusting both to his memory and to the subsequent experience or checking calculation that revealed the errors in question. Perhaps he need appeal only to the inconsistency between conflicting sense reports and diverging results of calculation. He need not make up his mind which is the correct result and which is the false one; he can content himself with observing that since the two contradict one at least must be false. But even for this he must continue to accept the principle that contradictories cannot both be true. Descartes, in fact, retains a large number of metaphysical principles, which he calls "principles of natural light." Among them are the principle that the efficient cause must contain at least as much reality as the effect and the proposition that creation is only notionally different from conservation (AT VII, 40, 49; HR I, 162, 168). Such principles, which seem at least as dubious as much that Descartes rejects, are not called in question even on the hypothesis of the evil genius. Indeed, as we shall see,

Descartes believed that to doubt them was impossible. Moreover, Descartes does not doubt that he knows the meaning of the words he uses to construct and resolve the doubts of the *Meditations*. In the *Principles* he admits that if the argument "I think, therefore I am" is to be able to resolve the universal doubt "we must first of all know what is knowledge, what is existence, and what is certainty and that in order to think we must be, and such like; but because these are notions of the simplest possible kind, which of themselves give us no knowledge of anything that exists, I did not think them worthy of being put on record" (AT VIII, 8; HR I, 222).

The scope, therefore, of Descartes' doubt is considerably less universal than it appears to be on first reading. A question also arises concerning the degree of seriousness with which he entertains his doubt. Does he ever *really* doubt the existence of God and the world? In the *Principles* he explains that the doubt is contemplative and not practical: ". . . we are to make use of this doubt only when we are engaged in contemplating the truth. For as regards the conduct of life, we are frequently obliged to follow opinions which are merely probable" (AT VIII, 5; HR I, 220). For instance, if we are not to die of hunger, we have to eat food without being certain that it is free from poison (Letter to Hyperaspistes, AT III, 398).

Nonetheless, the doubt is meant seriously. To Gassendi Descartes wrote: "My statement that the entire testimony of the senses must be considered to be uncertain, nay, even false, is quite serious and so necessary for the comprehension of my meditations that he who will not or cannot admit that, is unfit to urge any objection to them" (AT VII, 350; HR II, 206).

In the *Meditations* Descartes distinguishes between two different stages of doubt. His skeptical arguments convince him that none of his former ideas are beyond legitimate doubt: his opinions are no more than probable. To correct his natural bias toward regarding them as certain, he introduces the hypothesis of the evil genius. In making this supposition, he says, he is "deceiving himself" and is "pretending" that all his beliefs are wholly false and imaginary. In the *Principles*, too, he distinguishes between "calling into question" and "considering as false." It is natural to take this as a distinction between the suspension of judgment and actual disbelief; but this leads to an odd result. To disbelieve a proposition is to believe its contradictory. Thus, if Descartes means literally that he is going to consider all his former beliefs wholly false, he is not going to achieve his aim of avoiding falsehood. Among his former beliefs was the correct belief that he had a body. If he is going to reject this as false, then he is going to acquire the false belief that he has no body. This was pointed out by Gassendi and by the Jesuit Bourdin. "It is not certain that 2 and 3 make 5," wrote the latter. "Shall I then believe and affirm '2 and 3 do not make 5'?" Descartes replied indignantly:

> When I said that doubtful matters should sometimes be treated as though they were false, I clearly explained that I merely meant that, for the purpose of investigating the truths that are metaphysically certain, we should pay no more attention to doubtful matters than to what is plainly false. Thus surely no

sane man can interpret my words otherwise or attribute to me the opinion of wishing to believe the opposite of what is doubtful. (AT VII, 461; HR II, 266)

The last sentence is unfair to Bourdin, because the text of the *Meditations* is careless. But from Descartes' later explanations it is clear that he meant the distinction between "calling into question" and "rejecting as false" to be the distinction between hesitant belief and suspension of judgment, and not the distinction between suspension of judgment and positive disbelief. This coheres with his treating his previous beliefs as mere dreams. While I dream that Rome is burning, it may be, by a coincidence, that Rome is burning. Therefore, to decide that I am not really seeing Rome burning, but only dreaming that Rome is burning, is not *eo ipso* to decide that Rome is not burning.

Descartes' doubt about the existence of the world involves more than merely following up the consequences of the supposition that the world does not exist. Such an activity would be compatible with the retention of the most full-blooded belief in the world's existence. Yet, because the doubt finds no expression whatever in action, it is something less than a genuine suspension of belief. That is why Descartes could say in his synopsis of the *Meditations* that "no one of sound mind has ever doubted that there really is a world and that men have bodies" (AT VII, 16; HR I, 143).

Descartes sometimes calls his doubt "hyperbolical" and "metaphysical" (AT VII, 37, 90; HR I, 159, 199). By this he means that the suppositions on which the doubt depends—that life is a dream, that there is an omnipotent deceiver—are very improbable suppositions. They are, however, to be taken seriously to the extent that they are to be allowed to fill the mind. Until the proof of the existence and veracity of God shows them to be not only improbable but false, nothing is to be accepted as true that is incompatible with them. To correct the prejudices of his youth, Descartes is mentally to play the part of a man who believes the world does not exist. He is to think the thoughts that such a man would think. The doubt is, above all, a meditative technique, a form of thought therapy to cure the mind of excessive reliance on the senses. The cure may take a long time: the first meditation is to be dwelled upon for days and months.

In the contemplative order, the judgment that there is a world is to be genuinely withheld. Is this, we may ask, really possible? Even without acting accordingly, can one genuinely cease to believe that one has a body? Yes, says Descartes, for judgment and the suspension of judgment are acts not of the intellect but of the will. So long as the will is not compelled by a clear and distinct perception of a truth, it can make or withhold judgment as it pleases (AT VIII, 6; HR I, 221). In this case, the will is compelled neither by the prejudices of youth nor by the slender reasons for doubt; thus, using its liberty, the mind suspends judgment about the existence of the world.

As we have seen, Descartes carries out his program of doubt in several steps. First he casts doubt on the veracity of the senses. "I have sometimes caught the senses deceiving me; and a wise man never entirely trusts those who have once cheated him." No examples are given of sense deceptions in the *First Meditation*. The *Discourse* and the *Sixth Meditation* mention a number of phenomena familiar in skeptical literature. Square towers appear round from a distance; tall statues from afar seem tiny; distant stars look much smaller than they are; pain seems to be felt in an amputated limb. Not all these cases are strictly cases of the senses deceiving us; for to deceive is to induce a false belief, and it is possible for a tower to *look* round, or a star to *look* tiny, without my believing that the tower *is* round or the star *is* tiny. However, the examples are enough to show that not everything that appears to the senses to be the case actually is the case. And there certainly are cases, such as camouflage and mirages, where sense appearances do induce false beliefs.

But has Descartes the right to base a general mistrust on these special cases? Critics have argued that sense deception is only possible against a background of veridical perception. There cannot be errors, it is reasoned, where there is no possibility of correction, for if it makes no sense to talk of something's being corrected, then it makes no sense to talk of its being wrong. But if sense perceptions can be corrected, there must be some reliable sense perceptions to set the standard by which the correction is to be made. Thus, the sixth objectors said that when refraction made a stick half-immersed in water appear bent, the erroneous visual impression was corrected by the sense of touch (AT VII, 418; HR II, 238). Descartes seems to have accepted that a faculty that cannot be corrected cannot be in error; at least, in the *Third Meditation* he says that he cannot doubt what the natural light of reason shows to be true "because I possess no other faculty which can teach me that what this light shows to be true is not really true" (AT VII, 38; HR I, 161). But he did not agree with the sixth objectors that the errors of the senses were corrected by the senses themselves: it was the intellect that made the corrections. "Although it is owing to touch that we judge the stick to be straight . . . this is insufficient to correct the error. We need some reason in addition to show us why in this matter we ought to believe the tactile judgement rather than the visual one" (AT VII, 439; HR II, 253). This reply seems to show only that a veridical sense perception is not sufficient to correct a sense error, not that one is not necessary. But there are other cases where a deceptive sense perception of an object is corrected not by any further sense perception of that object, but by intellectual means alone. Thus, it is not by taking a closer look at the sun, but by understanding the reasons of astronomers, that I come to realize that the sun is larger than it looks (AT VII, 39; HR I, 161). And if I say that I could not even understand the astronomers' geometry unless I veraciously perceived the diagrams from which I learned geometry, Descartes can reply that the function of a triangle drawn on paper may merely be to awake my innate idea of a triangle, just as the strokes of a cartoonist may recall a human face (AT VII, 382; HR II, 228).

The theory of innate ideas also provides Descartes with a possible answer to another objection frequently made to the argument from sense illusions. Even to be deceived by the senses, it is said, we must understand the language in which they talk to us; just as I cannot be deceived by a lie in German if I know no German. Even to have a false belief that something is yellow, for example, one must know what yellow is; and how could one know this without having seen something that really was yellow? So do not fallacious sense perceptions presuppose veracious ones? In answer to this Descartes can agree that for a jaundiced man to think that snow is yellow, he must possess the idea of yellow. But why must he have acquired this idea from sensory contact with something truly yellow? May it not be an innate idea, implanted in his nature by God or the evil genius?

In fact, of course, Descartes *did* believe that the idea of yellow was innate. Moreover, he believed that *all* sensations of yellow—healthy perceptions of saffron, as well as jaundiced glimpses of snow—were deceptive insofar as they made the perceiver believe that something in the object perceived was similar to his sensation. The sensations of what Locke was later to call "secondary qualities"—colors, sounds, tastes, odors, heat, and the like—were all purely mental entities corresponding to nothing similar in reality (AT VIII, 322; HR I, 295). We shall discuss Descartes' reasons for this view when we discuss his theory of perception.

Now we note that as a result of it he regards the senses as deceptive in two different ways. Not being judgment, sense perception is strictly neither true nor false; the will, not the sense of sight, judges the half-immersed stick to be bent. But the senses are deceptive in that they lead us to judge (1) that there are things in the world like secondary qualities, and (2) that objects in the world have certain primary qualities—size, shape, position—that are other than the ones they really have. Given the strategy of the *Meditations*, Descartes cannot appeal to the universal falsity of judgments of type (1) in order to persuade the reader to doubt his senses; this is one of the conclusions to which he hopes to lead the reader once purified by Cartesian doubt. Instead, he appeals to the occasional falsity represented by judgments of type (2). He draws his examples from errors concerning the shape, size, and distance of objects perceived by sense. In the *Discourse*, but not in the *Meditations*, he mentioned the alleged optical effects of jaundice. But a man who believes that nothing is ever really colored cannot honestly appeal to the fact that things sometimes appear to have a color different from the one they have in reality.

The skepticism of the *First Meditation*, I have argued, cannot be refuted by the contention that deceptive sense perception presupposes veracious sense perception unless that contention is reinforced by a critique of the theory of innate ideas. On the other hand, the premise that the senses sometimes mislead us about qualities cannot by itself lead to the conclusion that it is possible that they always mislead us. Neither in the *First Meditation* nor in the *Sixth Meditation* does Descartes suggest that it can. In the *First Meditation* he puts to himself the objection, "although the senses sometimes deceive us about some minute or remote objects, yet there are many other facts as to which doubt is plainly impossible." To this objection he does not offer any reply drawn from the field of deceptive sense appearances, but introduces a new argument concerning delusions and dreams.

First, he considers the possibility that his current sense impressions may be no more than the delusions of a madman. The question "How do I know that I am not mad?" is one of great philosophical interest. It is not pursued, possibly because it might seem offensive to the reader (AT X, 510; HR I, 314), but is replaced by the question "How do I know that I am not dreaming?"

Descartes' statement that there appears to be no criterion by which we can tell dreams from waking experiences has been much criticized. The late J. L. Austin maintained in a lecture that there were about fifty such criteria. In the published version of the lecture, *Sense and Sensibilia*, we read, "I may have the experience . . . of dreaming that I am being presented to the Pope. Could it be seriously suggested that having this dream is 'qualitatively indistinguishable' from *actually being* presented to the Pope? Quite obviously not." [1] Indeed, Descartes himself offers in the *Sixth Meditation* a distinguishing criterion: "Dreams are never connected by memory with all the other events of my life, like the things which happen when I am awake." But this criterion, he thinks, needs to be supplemented by an appeal to the veracity of God (AT VII, 89; HR I, 199).

Norman Malcolm believes that both Descartes and Austin are looking for an answer to a nonsensical question.

The famous philosophical question "How can I tell whether I am awake or dreaming?" turns out to be quite senseless since it implies that it is possible to judge that one is dreaming and this judgement is as unintelligible as the judgement that one is asleep. Furthermore the question appears to presuppose that one might be able to tell that one is dreaming, which is double nonsense: for this would mean that one made an inherently unintelligible judgement while asleep.[2]

It seems to me that the question "Am I awake or am I dreaming?" is not senseless, if that means that it has no possible answer. For there is a true answer to the question—namely, "I am awake." Moreover, I know this answer. If I am asked *how* I know it, however, I can give no answer. I can give no grounds for the assertion. There is no fact better known to me than the fact that I am awake, that I can offer as a reason for saying that I am awake. When I say "I am awake," I do so without grounds, but not without justification.

I can give no grounds for my assertion that I am awake, for whatever grounds I give will be at least as much open to doubt as the assertion that I am awake. Let the reason I give be *p*. Then the skeptic can always ask, "How do you know that you are not merely dreaming that *p*?" To this extent the skeptical Descartes is correct. But as Hobbes pointed out, this applies also when *p* is: "My memory is uniting the events which are happening to me to the whole course of my life" (AT VII, 195; HR II, 78). So the criterion of the *Sixth Meditation* fails, in spite of the veracity of God.

Descartes says, "I never have believed myself to feel anything in waking moments which I cannot also sometimes believe myself to feel when I sleep" (AT VII, 78; HR I, 189). This seems wrong. To dream that something is the case is not to believe that something is the case. I agree with Malcolm against Descartes that one cannot make judgments during dreams. It does not follow, however, that the judgment "I am dreaming" is senseless. It can never be made truly, but it can be made falsely. To dream that one is dreaming is not to judge that one is dreaming, but a waking man might be persuaded falsely to judge that he is dreaming.

The judgment "I am awake" cannot be mistaken. "But can't I dream that I am awake?" Descartes objects. Yes, but to dream that I am awake is not to judge that I am awake. It is impossible falsely to believe that one is awake, because one cannot entertain beliefs in sleep. In contrast to "I am dreaming," the judgment "I am awake" can only be made truly, never falsely. The question "Am I awake?" is not senseless; it is pointless only to the extent that if a man is in a position to ask the question, he is also in a position to answer it.

The skeptical Descartes, then, is right in thinking that "Am I awake or dreaming?" is a genuine question. He is right also in suggesting in the *First Meditation* that there is no criterion by which we answer this question. But he is wrong in thinking that it follows that we cannot know the answer to the question. Moreover, he cannot reject the claim that we know some things without being able to give any grounds for our knowledge, for he himself thinks that in this way we know the nature of our own thoughts. We do not know whether they are waking or sleeping thoughts, but we know what *kind* of thoughts they are. "I am now seeing light, hearing a noise, feeling heat. These objects are unreal, for I am asleep; but at least I seem to see, to hear, to be warmed. This cannot be unreal" (AT VII, 29; HR I, 153).

The argument about dreaming leads only to a

modest skepticism. It calls in doubt all particular sense beliefs and the existence of composite tangible objects, but it leaves intact the claim that "there are some other objects more simple and more universal which are real and true." As examples of these simple universals, Descartes mentions "corporeal nature in general and its extension, shape, size, number, duration"; out of these are formed "all the images of things which dwell in our thoughts, whether true and real or false and fantastic."

The items listed in the *First Meditation* correspond to the simple natures of the twelfth *Rule for the Direction of the Mind*. Simplicity is there explained as unanalyzability.

> Take a body that has shape and extension. We shall admit that objectively there is one simple fact; we cannot call it, in this sense, "a compound of the natures *body, extension,* and *figure*", for these "parts" have never existed separate from one another. But in respect of our understanding we do call it a compound of these three natures; for we had to understand each one separately before judging that the three are found in one and the same subject . . . We use the term "simple" only for realities so clearly and distinctly known that we cannot divide any of them into several realities more distinctly known, for example, shape, extension, motion, etc.; and we conceive of everything else as somehow compounded out of these. (AT X, 418; HR I, 40–41)

In the *Rules*, the knowledge of these simple natures is infallible (AT X, 420; HR I, 42); in the *Meditations* it is not called in question by the supposition that life is a dream.

Arithmetic, Geometry and other sciences of that kind
which treat only of things that are very simple and
very general without caring to ascertain whether they
exist in nature or not, contain some measure of indubitable certainty. . . . For whether I am awake
or asleep, two and three together always make five.
(AT VII, 420; HR I, 147)

Two things are surprising about this statement.
First, the two reasons given for the indubitability of
mathematics—that its objects are simple and that they
need not exist—do not seem equivalent, and the second
seems inappropriate to the context. Second, as Bourdin
pointed out, it is surely possible to dream that two and
three make six (AT VII, 457; HR II, 263-264).

The answer to the first difficulty is that existence
is itself a simple nature (AT X, 418; HR I, 41). For a
simple nature to exist is precisely for it to be combined
with another simple nature, namely, existence. In the
case of everything except God, this combination will be
contingent and not necessary. Therefore it will be no
concern of any science that studies simple natures and
their necessary connections. Created existents are all
composite. Simple natures can be studied whether or
not they exist.

The answer Descartes gave to the second difficulty
was that though a dreamer could *think* he was clearly
and distinctly perceiving that two and three are six, he
could not really be doing so (AT VII, 462; HR II, 267).
But this answer seems inadequate. Could I not with as
much right say that in a dream I only think I perceive
that I am sitting by the fire, that I do not really perceive myself doing so? The argument from dreaming

seems to be either insufficient to call in question sense perception, or else sufficient to call in question mathematics. Descartes, however, offers quite a different hypothesis for this purpose.

God is said to be all-powerful. May He not therefore have brought it about that I am deceived, not only in sense perception of earth and sky, but also in my understanding of the simple natures of extension, size, and place, and in my performance of the simplest arithmetical operations?

Some will prefer to think that there is no omnipotent God than that everything is uncertain. But if the cause of my being is less than omnipotent, the greater will be the probability that I am so imperfect as to deceive myself always.

Notice that the answer to the objection involves an astonishing *volte face*. First, the production of delusive perception and understanding is regarded as a fraud so gigantic that nothing less than omnipotence can be thought of as perpetrating it. Then the viewpoint is switched from that of the deceiver to that of the person deceived. From this point of view the deception is treated as a defect that calls for no positive explanation at all.

No sooner has the hypothesis of the deceitful God been proposed than it is replaced by the hypothesis of the evil genius. Henri Gouhier has argued that these two hypotheses are fundamentally distinct in purpose and in content.

The first hypothesis arises from an intellectual scruple; it is metaphysical in nature and disappears when metaphysics demonstrates its falsity. The second is a methodological procedure operated by the will and imagination in order to make a certain experiment; it ceases with that experiment. The deceitful God is a possible existent whom I do not yet know; it is perhaps the true God confusedly discerned. The evil genius is an artificial device with no pretensions to existence, whose essence is in no way mysterious to me since I am its author. Neither the purpose nor the content of the two hypotheses allow us to regard the one as a variant of the other.[3]

In fact, the two hypotheses do not differ in any respect of epistemological importance. The hypothesis of the evil genius is substituted for that of the deceitful God simply because it is less offensive and less patently incoherent. The content of the two hypotheses is the same, namely, that an omnipotent deceiver is trying to deceive Descartes in every way in which it is possible for him to be deceived. The purpose of taking seriously the hypothesis of the evil genius is to counterbalance natural credulity and keep in mind the doubts raised by the supposition of the deceitful God. "I shall therefore suppose, not that God who is supremely good and the source of truth, but that some evil genius of supreme power and intelligence, has employed his whole energies to deceive me."

It is the "therefore" in this passage that has led people to believe that the hypothesis of the evil genius is to serve a more radically skeptical purpose than the hypothesis of the deceitful God. But Descartes at this point is not adopting a completely novel hypothesis; he is taking up a new attitude to an equivalent hypothesis. What he has hitherto considered as possible—namely,

that he is the prey of an omnipotent deceiver—he will
henceforth pretend is true. The evil genius in the
quoted sentence is contrasted not with the hypothetical deceitful God, but with the yet unproved veracious
God. The evil genius calls nothing in doubt that had
not already been called in doubt by the hypothesis of
the divine deceit. If the two hypotheses differ at all, it
is the first that is more skeptical than the second. God,
Descartes suggested, may have made him go wrong in
mathematics and all that seemed most simple; the evil
genius merely reinforces the doubt that the external
world may be a dream. "I will suppose that sky, air,
earth, colours, shapes, sounds and all external objects
are mere delusive dreams by means of which he lays
snares for my credulity." There is no word here of any
doubt about the simple natures or the axioms of mathematics.

Is the hypothesis of an omnipotent deceiver coherent? Let us leave aside the reason Descartes later offers
for its refutation, namely, that it is incompatible with
the existence of a veracious, benevolent, and omnipotent God. Is there anything else wrong with it?

Objections have been brought to the hypothesis
from two quarters: analytic empiricism and scholastic
rationalism. O. K. Bouwsma has argued that if the evil
genius is to deceive as Descartes says, then the evil
genius must create an illusion of such a kind that no
seeing, no touching, no sensing is relevant to the detection of the illusion. But if the evil genius is to create
the illusion, he must detect the illusion; he can do this
only by means of some mode of perception that is denied to man. But in that case what he creates are not
illusions. "For human beings do not use the word 'illu-

sion' by reference to a sense with which only the evil genius is blessed." [4]

It is clear from the *Sixth Replies* how Descartes would have replied to this criticism. Even human beings, he would claim, discover illusions not by means of a sense, but by the use of the intellect; there is, therefore, no need to consider the omnipotent deceiver either to be endowed with a sense faculty or to mean something different from us if he speaks of an "illusion" (AT VII, 439; HR II, 253).

To a traditional scholastic, the hypothesis presented a different difficulty. According to Aquinas, even omnipotence is limited by necessary truths. "Whatever implies contradiction," he wrote, "does not come within the scope of divine omnipotence because it cannot have the aspect of possibility." [5] If I can be sure, then, that the contradictory of a proposition implies a contradiction, I can be certain of that proposition; for not even omnipotence can make its contradictory come true. Thus, necessary truths cannot be tampered with even by an omnipotent deceiver or by God himself. This point was made by the authors of the *Sixth Objections*.

> How can the truths of geometry and metaphysics such as you mention be immutable and eternal, and yet not be independent of God? What possible action of God's could annul the nature of the triangle, and how could he from all eternity bring it to pass that it was untrue that twice four was eight or that a triangle had not three angles? (AT VII, 418; HR II, 238)

Descartes, however, believed—not just as a methodological hypothesis, but as a metaphysical principle—that the truths of geometry and arithmetic were dependent on the free will of God. "The mathematical truths," he wrote to Mersenne, "which you call eternal, were established by God and depend on him entirely, just like all other creatures" (AT I, 145). God, he wrote again, "was as free to make it not be true that all the radii of a circle were equal as he was free not to create the world" (AT I, 152). To Arnauld he wrote later that we should not say that God could not make it be the case that two and one did not equal three; but simply that He had given us the kind of mind that could not conceive of an aggregate of two and one that was not equal to three (AT V, 226). He would not have been distressed, therefore, by arguments against the evil genius drawn from the limits laid on omnipotence by necessary truths.[6]

Many of the problems raised by the *First Meditation* cannot be treated until we see how Descartes himself resolved his doubts. But it is notable how much of Cartesian metaphysics is latent in the arguments for Cartesian doubt. In the course of our discussion we have encountered the notions of innate ideas and indubitable simple natures, the theories of the natural light of the intellect and the judging power of the will, the doctrines of the subjectivity of secondary qualities, and the creation of eternal truths. These theses are not exactly presupposed by Descartes' skeptical arguments but they are positions he must fall back upon in order to defend them against objection. This observation does not refute the skepticism of the *First Meditation*: as Descartes pointed out to Bourdin, an argument need not itself be certain in order to show that something else is less than certain (AT VII, 474; HR II, 277). But it does greatly weaken the force of the arguments as a persuasive tool.

They are presented in the *Meditations* as if they were arguments that anyone, Cartesian or non-Cartesian, must admit to be true; and the Cartesian system is then presented as the only means of rescue from the morass of doubt to which the arguments lead. If I am right, however, the skeptical arguments gain their full force only if the reader is prepared to entertain the Cartesian system as possible from the outset; they leave him the option of refusing to consider it at all. The challenge Descartes presents to the reader amounts to this: "How can you prove the falsehood of my entire system of innate ideas of simple indubitable natures linked by the arbitrary will of an omnipotent God?"

THREE

COGITO ERGO SUM

Descartes' doubt is at last halted by the certainty of his own existence. His proof of this is summed up in the three words "*cogito ergo sum*," which must have called forth a million times their number in commentary. They occur first in the *Discourse*.

> I noticed that while I was trying to think everything false, it must needs be that I, who was thinking this, was something. And observing that this truth "I am thinking, therefore I exist" was so solid and secure that the most extravagant suppositions of the sceptics could not overthrow it, I judged that I need not scruple to accept it as the first principle of philosophy that I was seeking. (AT VII, 32; HR I, 101)

In the fullest treatment of the topic, in the *Second Meditation*, the famous catch phrase does not occur; but it returns in the *Principles of Philosophy* and *The Search After Truth*.

I have called the *cogito* a proof. It has always been debated whether it was intended as an argument or as an appeal to intuition. "Ergo" is the mark of an argument; and Descartes calls his adage a "reasoning" (AT X, 523; HR I, 324) and says that his existence "follows from" his thinking of doubting (AT VI, 32; HR I, 101) and calls the "sum" a conclusion (AT VIII, 8; HR I, 222). On the other hand, in reply to the *Second Objections*, Descartes wrote:

> When we observe that we are thinking beings, this is a sort of primary notion, which is not the conclusion of any syllogism; and, moreover, when somebody says: I am thinking, therefore I am or exist, he is not using a syllogism to deduce his existence from his thought, but recognizing this as something self-evident, in a simple mental intuition. (AT VII, 140; HR II, 38)

Even if we take this text as decisive, there is no agreement about the sense of "intuition." Some have interpreted it as an act of introspection; thus Chevalier writes that Descartes founds his whole philosophy on an immediate datum of conscious experience.[1] Others have interpreted it as the recognition of the self-confirmatory character of an utterance such as "I think." Thus, A. J. Ayer writes: "What makes them [sc. 'I think' and 'I exist'] indubitable is their satisfying a condition which Descartes himself does not make explicit, though his argument turns upon it. It is that their truth follows from their being doubted by the person who expresses them." [2] The former view is perhaps more common on the continent; the latter within the Anglo-American tradition. It is a consequence of either interpretation that the *"cogito"* is in a sense superfluous: the *"sum"* is reached directly and not via the *"cogito."** Thus, Chevalier speaks of Descartes' intuition, which "reveals the fact of his existence with a vital clarity." And Ayer says "There was therefore no need for Descartes to derive *'sum'* from *'cogito'*; for its certainty could be independently established by the same criterion." In support of this view it is pointed out that in the *Rules* Descartes, without bringing in *"cogito"* as a premise, says "Everyone can intuit that he exists."

Jaakko Hintikka has recently made a very thorough attempt to do justice both to the inferential aspect of the *cogito* and to its intuitive aspect interpreted in terms of self-confirmation.[3] There are, he believes, two different arguments compressed into the *cogito*. In the first, Descartes treats the dictum as an instance of a logical truth to the effect that if an individual possesses an attribute, then that individual exists. "I am thinking, therefore I am," on this interpretation, differs from "I am walking, therefore I am" only because its premise is more indubitable. Thus interpreted, Hintikka believes, the *cogito* is invalid. Hamlet had many thoughts, Hintikka argues, but Hamlet did not exist.

The second argument turns on what Hintikka calls the "existential self-verifiability" of the sentence "I

---

* When *"cogito"* appears thus, in quotation marks, it refers to the premise of the *"cogito ergo sum"*; when I speak of the *cogito*, I mean the dictum as a whole.

exist." The sentence "I exist" verifies itself whenever it is uttered or otherwise put forward. In the same way, the sentence "I don't exist" is self-defeating, since if anyone uses it to try to persuade anyone, including himself, of its truth, he defeats his own purpose. On this interpretation, Hintikka says, "the function of the word 'cogito' in Descartes' dictum is to refer to the thought-act through which the existential self-verifiability of 'I exist' manifests itself." The thought-act in question is the final step in the Cartesian doubt: the attempt to convince himself that he does not exist. It is the self-defeating nature of this attempt which reveals the self-verifiability of "I exist." The relation, then, of "*cogito*" to "*sum*" is not that of premise to conclusion; rather, the indubitability of my own existence results from my thinking of it somewhat as the sound of music may result from my playing it. The *cogito* is not an inference, but a performance.

Despite his ingenuity and scholarship, Hintikka fails to carry conviction. It seems barely credible that two such different arguments should be so compressed and confused in Descartes' thought that it should be impossible to tell whether a particular instance of the *cogito* is an inference or a performance. On Hintikka's interpretation, Descartes, in every presentation of the *cogito* outside the *Meditations*, leaves out of his proof an element essential to its validity: that the thought referred to by the word "*cogito*" is a thought about his own existence. He has to admit that even in the *Meditations* Descartes chooses the wrong words to express his fundamental insight; for the existential inconsistency on which the argument is alleged to turn arises not from

Descartes' attempt to doubt his existence, but from his attempt to *profess to himself* that he does not exist. Strictly, Hintikka thinks, Descartes ought to have concluded "*ego sum professor*" rather than "*sum res cogitans.*"[4] It is surely preferable, if possible, to find some interpretation of the *cogito* that will make Descartes appear less thoroughly confused.[5]

One of the difficulties that Hintikka's interpretation entails is an ambiguity in the sense of "*cogito.*" If we take the *cogito* as an inference, then the word "*cogito*" can be taken in a broad sense to refer to any act of consciousness; *cogito ergo sum* is on the same footing with such arguments as *volo ergo sum*. But if we take the *cogito* as a performance, then the verb must be taken in a very precise sense as a "verb of intellection," a verb apt to report the attempt to persuade oneself that one does not exist; "think" or "doubt," perhaps, but not "will" or "feel."

Whenever Descartes sets out to explain what he means by "*cogitare*," he always gives the verb a much wider sense than that of the English verb "to think." Thus, when he sets out his system axiomatically, *more geometrico*, in an appendix to his answers to the *Second Objections*, he gives as his first definition the following: "*Thought (cogitatio, pensée)* is a word that covers everything that exists in us in such a way that we are immediately aware of it. Thus, all the operations of will, intellect, imagination, and of the senses are thoughts."

And in the *Principles* Descartes explains:

Suppose I say *I see* (or *I am walking*) *therefore I exist*. If I take this to refer to vision (or walking) as a corporeal action, the conclusion is not absolutely cer-

tain; for, as often happens during sleep, I may think
I am seeing though I do not open my eyes (or think
I am walking although I do not change my place);
and it may even be that I have no body. But if I take
it to refer to the actual sensation or consciousness of
seeing (or walking) then it is quite certain; for in
that case it has regard to the mind, and it is the
mind alone that has a sense or thought of itself seeing (or walking). (AT VIII, 8; HR I, 222)

"*Cogito*," therefore, can be used to cover a wide
range of mental activities. There seems no indication
that in order to serve as a premise for the *cogito ergo
sum* it has to be taken in a restricted manner. In the
Meditations, indeed, Descartes does seem to derive his
existence from thoughts in the narrow sense: the
thought that there is no world, the thought that I
exist. The deceiver "will never bring it about that at
the time of thinking (*quamdiu cogitabo*) that I am
something, I am in fact nothing" (AT VII, 25; HR I,
150). But even here Descartes at once adds something
that takes us beyond pure thought: "The proposition
(*pronunciatum*) 'I am', 'I exist', whenever I utter it or
conceive it in my mind, is necessarily true." How can
Descartes know that he is *uttering* the proposition "I
exist" when he is still in doubt whether he has a body
with lips, tongue, and teeth? "I am uttering 'I exist,'
therefore I am." The premise here is indubitable only
if it refers to the sensation or impression of uttering "I
exist." And this impression will be a *cogitatio* in the
wide sense.

In various places Descartes says that conscious acts
of the most diverse kinds are capable of providing premises for the *cogito*: "I try to think everything false" (AT

VI, 32; HR I, 101); "We doubt of the truth of all these things (God, heaven, earth, body)" (AT VIII, 7; HR I, 221); "I think that I am walking" (AT VII, 352; HR II, 207); "I feel that I am breathing" (AT II, 34 ff.); "I seem to see" (AT VIII, 7; HR I, 222). Indeed, in the *Principles* Descartes seems to say that any cognitive act whatever will serve.

> There is nothing that gives rise to knowledge of any object, which does not even more certainly lead us to know our thought. For instance, if I persuade myself that there is an earth because I touch or see it, by that very fact, and for much better reason, I should be persuaded that my thought exists, because it may be that I think I touch the earth even though there is possibly no earth in existence at all, but it is not possible that I—that is, my soul—should be non-existent while it has this thought. We can draw the same conclusion from all the other things which come into our thought; namely, that we who think them exist. (AT VIII, 9; HR I, 223)

These considerations seem conclusive against Hintikka's account and indeed against any self-confirmatory interpretation of the *cogito*. Expounding such an interpretation, Ayer argues: "If I believe that I am thinking, then I must believe truly, since my believing that I am thinking is itself a process of thought." But one could not argue similarly: "If I think I am touching the earth, then I must think truly, since my thinking that I am touching the earth is itself a process of touching the earth." In fact, it is clear that the possibility of a thought remaining a thought even when *false* is what makes it suitable as a premise for the *cogito* (AT II, 34 ff.).

For Hintikka it is essential to the validity of the performative *cogito* that the thought in question should be a thought about Descartes' own existence. But Descartes gives at least seven examples of other *cogitationes* that will do as well, and he suggests that there is no limit to the number of examples that might be supplied. Again, it is essential to the performatory interpretation that the *cogito* be a proof that each man can go through for himself only. But Descartes states the proof not only in the first person singular (*Discourse, Meditations*), but also in the first person plural (*Principles*) and in the second person (*Search After Truth*). In the *Principles*, as Hintikka himself points out, Descartes observes in the third person that "there is a contradiction in conceiving that what thinks does not, at the same time as it thinks, exist."

All this comes out very clearly in what was perhaps Descartes' longest single exposition of the *cogito*, the dialogue entitled *The Search After Truth*. Eudoxus, the exponent of Descartes' method, says to Polyander, the plain man: "You see that you can reasonably doubt all things, the knowledge of which comes to you by the sense alone; but can you doubt of your doubt and remain uncertain whether you doubt or not?" Polyander agrees that he doubts and is certain of nothing. Eudoxus goes on: "Since then you cannot deny that you doubt, and it is on the contrary certain that you doubt, and so certain that you cannot doubt of it, it is likewise true that you who doubt exist, and this is so true that you can no longer doubt of it." And Polyander agrees: "I agree with you, for if I did not exist I could not doubt" (AT X, 515; HR I, 316).

In this passage, Descartes is insisting on the certainty of the premise "*dubito*." This premise cannot be regarded, in any simple way, as self-confirmatory; it is not something like "I exist," which is true whenever it is uttered. Nor is there anything self-refuting about the statement "I have no doubts." There is, however, a peculiarity about the statement "I doubt whether I doubt." For from "I doubt whether there is something that I doubt," I can infer "there is something that I doubt." This is simply a matter of quantification theory, an instance of existential generalization, a form of inference exemplified when we pass from "I love Mary," to "I love someone." [6] But this does not mean that my doubt is itself indubitable. It means rather that it contains its own solution. If I know that I doubt whether I doubt, then I know enough to resolve the doubt. But this does not prevent me from doubting that I doubt, unless it is also the case that if I doubt then I know that I doubt. But if we can add the extra premise "If I doubt, I know that I doubt," then we can show the indubitability of my doubt without appealing to the self-resolving nature of the doubt that I doubt. For if whenever I doubt I know that I doubt, then I cannot doubt whether I doubt, since one cannot doubt what one knows (AT VII, 473; HR II, 276).

In the passage cited, Descartes does indeed ask, "Can you doubt of your doubt and be uncertain whether you doubt or not?" The question expects and gets the answer no. But there is no suggestion in the text that the negative answer is based on any appeal to the self-resolving nature of such a doubt. There is, on the other hand, much to suggest that it is based on the premise "whoever doubts knows that he doubts." Eudoxus says that it is because Polyander cannot *deny* that he doubts that he cannot doubt that he doubts. But, as we have seen, there is nothing self-refuting in the denial of one's doubt: Eudoxus cannot deny his doubt simply because it is obvious to him. Eudoxus says, a little further on, "You exist, and you know that you exist, and you know that because you doubt." Four lines later he says, "Let us repeat the argument: you exist, and you know that you exist, and you know that because you know that you doubt." In saying this, Eudoxus is using "you doubt" and "you know that you doubt" as interchangeable. This is most readily intelligible if Descartes believed that one doubted if and only if one knew that one doubted. What reason can be found in his system for such a belief?

The answer is obvious. Doubting is one kind of thought; and thought is defined precisely as "whatever takes place within ourselves so that we are conscious of it, in so far as it is an object of our consciousness." Therefore, "if I doubt I know that I doubt" follows, for Descartes, from the definition he has given of thought, of which doubting is a species or mode. We might say that according to Descartes' definition, if we wish to find whether a given verb ϕ, which is applied to human beings, signifies a kind of thought or not, we must ask "is it true that when I ϕ I know that I ϕ?" Descartes therefore makes it true by definition that if I think, I know that I think. It is here that the indubitability of the premise of "*cogito ergo sum*" is to be found.

This, of course, is not how Descartes would have put it. He thought it unnecessary to define "thought" in order to make the *cogito* conclude. Critics objected that the *cogito* could not be the first principle of philosophy since it presupposed the knowledge of what thought, doubt, and existence were. With the substance of this criticism, Descartes always agreed. But, he said, this knowledge can be presupposed in everyone. It is not a question of knowing how to define thought and existence *per genus et differentiam* in the manner of the schools. To know what doubt and thought are it is enough to doubt and to think: this teaches us all we can know in this respect and even tells us more than the most exact definitions (AT VIII, 8; HR I, 222). What thought is, he wrote, is "so self-evident that there is nothing more evident which can be used to explain it" (Letter to Hyperaspistes, AT IV, 426). He believed, of course, that the idea of thought was innate; but he did not need to rely on this in reply to his critics (AT VII, 38; HR I, 160).

Understanding the nature of thought would involve a further insight that Descartes admitted to be necessary as a preliminary to the *cogito*. "We must know," he said in the *Principles*, "such things as that it is impossible for that which is thinking to be non-existent; but I thought it needless to enumerate these notions, for they are of the greatest simplicity, and by themselves they can give us no knowledge that anything exists" (AT VIII, 8; HR I, 222). "To think, one must exist" appears to be a particular instance of a general principle that Descartes says is manifest by natural light in our souls, namely, that "nothing has no qualities or properties, so that where we perceive some there must necessarily be a thing or substance on which they depend" (AT VIII, 8; HR I, 223).

We are now in a position to see the structure of the *cogito*. At any moment when Descartes is engaged in a conscious activity—say, when he is thinking, doubting, willing, or sensing—the proposition "*cogito*" is true. Because thought is by definition known to its agent, the proposition is not only true, but also indubitable to Descartes; for what is known cannot be doubted (AT VII, 473; HR II, 276). The premise "*cogito*" in conjunction with the presupposition that it is impossible for that which is thinking to be nonexistent yield the conclusion "*sum*." Since the premise is indubitable, and the conclusion follows from it by the light of nature, the conclusion too is indubitable.

The argument as just interpreted could be formulated in a simple syllogism, provided we are willing to follow Descartes in regarding "exists" as a predicate (AT VII, 382; HR II, 228). "Whatever is thinking exists; but I am thinking; therefore I exist." What then are we to make of Descartes' denial, in reply to the *Second Objections*, that the *cogito* is the conclusion of a syllogism?

The question was put to Descartes in 1648 by Burman, who pointed out that the statement in the *Second Replies* appeared to contradict the passage quoted above from the *Principles*. Descartes replied:

> Before the conclusion "I am thinking, therefore I am" it is possible to know the major: "whatever is thinking exists", because in reality it is prior to my conclusion and my conclusion rests upon it. That is why in the *Principles* the author says that it precedes it, because implicitly it is always presupposed and prior. But I do not always have an express and ex-

plicit knowledge of this priority, and I know my conclusion first, because I pay attention only to what I
observe in my own case, namely, "I am thinking,
therefore I exist" and do not pay equal attention to
the general axiom "whatever is thinking, exists". Indeed, as I have pointed out, we do not separate such
propositions from individual things, but we take note
of them in the particular case. (AT V, 147)

This is not altogether clear. It seems odd, to begin
with, that Descartes should call "I am thinking, therefore I exist" a conclusion, when in fact it is a minor
premise plus a conclusion; or, in spite of the contrast
with "the major," does he in fact mean by "conclusion"
the *drawing of* a conclusion, that is, an inference? Perhaps what he means is this: the inference from "*cogito*"
to "*sum*" is a valid inference only if "whatever is thinking, exists" is true. But before going through the *cogito*
I may never have thought of the general proposition.
Drawing the conclusion "*sum*" from the premise "*cogito*" is one possible exercise of the knowledge that whatever thinks exists. In drawing the conclusion, therefore,
I may be said to display such knowledge. But if so, we
must add that the knowledge is implicit, since I have
never considered the proposition before. It may be precisely in drawing the conclusion in the particular case
that I first come to realize the general truth. As Descartes said in his answer to the *Second Objections*:

The major premise, that everything that thinks is, or
exists, would have to be known previously; but yet
that has rather been learned from the experience of
the individual, that unless he exists he cannot think.
For our mind is so constituted by nature that general

propositions are formed out of the knowledge of particulars. (AT VII, 140; HR II, 38)

And to Clerselier he wrote:

In order to discover the truth one must assuredly begin with particular notions, and then go on to general ones afterwards; although, conversely, after having discovered the general notions, one can likewise deduce further particular notions from them. For example, when a child is taught the elements of geometry, he cannot be made to understand in general that if from equal quantities equal parts are subtracted the remainders are still equal, or that the whole is greater than its parts, unless he is shown examples in particular cases. (AT IX, 205; HR II, 127)

On the account I have given it is plain why Descartes should have called the *cogito* a piece of reasoning. But what are we to make of the passages in which it appears to be presented as an intuition? Sometimes, what is presented as the object of the intuition is not the proposition "*sum*" but the whole adage "*cogito ergo sum.*" Thus, in a famous letter to the Marquis of Newcastle Descartes wrote:

. . . you will surely admit that you are less assured of the presence of the objects you see than of the truth of the proposition "I think, therefore I am"? Now this knowledge is no product of your reasoning, no lesson that your masters have taught you; it is something that your mind sees, feels, handles. (AT V, 137)

Here it is not knowledge of his own existence that is being described as intuitive; it is knowledge of what is expressed by the whole *cogito*. The denial that "I am thinking, therefore I am" is the conclusion of an inference is perfectly compatible with its being itself an inference. The most difficult passage is the one from the *Second Replies*, which Haldane and Ross translate thus: "He who says 'I think, hence I am or exist' does not deduce existence from thought by a syllogism, but by a simple act of mental vision, recognizes it as if it were a thing that is known *per se*." The "it" is not in the Latin text, and as that text stands it is ambiguous what exactly is known *per se*. Hintikka maintains that it is *"sum"*; Weinberg has argued that it is the whole *cogito*, or perhaps rather the connection between existence and thought.[7] Hintikka quotes against this the French version of Clerselier; but the French text is equally ambiguous, though in a different manner. Even if Hintikka is right, Descartes merely says that existence is known *as if* it is self-evident, not that it *is* self-evident.[8] The truth of *"sum"* is not self-evident independently of the truth of *"cogito,"* but is seen as self-evidently contained in it.

In the *Rules*, however, there is no doubt that Descartes says that everyone can intuit his own existence, without suggesting that *"cogito"* is needed as a premise. This, however, was written before the enunciation of the *cogito*, which it is surely reasonable to regard as a precise statement of the insight obscurely formulated in the *Rules*. Moreover, the *Rules* themselves bring support to our interpretation when they assert that "the evidentness and certainty of intuition is moreover necessary not only in forming propositions, but also for any inferences." Intuition is necessary not only for seeing the truth of premises, but for seeing that conclusions follow from premises, so that what is from one point of view intuited is from another point of view deduced (AT X, 370; HR I, 8). The intuition in the *cogito*, if I am right, is not the intuition of existence, but the intuition that the conclusion follows from the premise.

It seems possible, therefore, to settle the debate about whether the *cogito* is an intuition or an inference. Those who look upon it as an inference are correct insofar as *"ergo"* is genuinely a mark of the drawing of a conclusion, and the truth and indubitability of the premise *"cogito"* is a necessary, and not a superfluous, step toward establishing the truth and indubitability of the conclusion *"sum."* Those who think of the *cogito* as an appeal to introspection are right in that the indubitability of the premise *"cogito"* results from its truth only because thought is by definition something of which the thinker is immediately conscious. Those who claim that the *cogito* is performative have this much truth, that the particular event that makes the premise *"cogito"* true may be a mental performance; but it need not be, and a headache will do just as well.

As long as I exist, Descartes believed, the proposition *"cogito"* is true of me; the particular *cogitationes* that make it true vary from moment to moment, from dim prenatal pleasures to metaphysical meditations. But not every verb that we might regard as reporting an episode in a man's mental life will do as a premise for the *cogito*. Take, for instance, "I am dreaming." Why does Descartes never say, "I am dreaming, therefore I exist"? It might seem a natural way out of a muddle into which he has got himself by wondering whether he was awake or dreaming. But it is clear that "I am dreaming, therefore I exist" is useless to him because its premise is so uncertain. One can dream without knowing that one is dreaming; "I am dreaming" therefore does not, on Descartes' definition, record the occurrence of a *cogitatio*. Nor can he argue, "I am awake, therefore I exist," since he believes that one can, while awake, be in doubt whether one may not be dreaming. Sleep and waking life, though they consist of thoughts, are not themselves thoughts. Certainly a dreamer can prove his own existence by means of a *cogito*, but he cannot use the fact that he is dreaming as its premise; he must appeal to some particular experience in his dream, such as seeming to see a white rabbit.

Descartes' argument for his existence in the *Second Meditation* has a more complicated structure than the *cogito* presented elsewhere:[9]

> I myself, am not I at least something? But I have already denied that I have senses and body. Yet I hesitate, for what follows from that? Am I so tied to body and senses that without them I cannot exist? But I persuaded myself that there was nothing in all the world, no sky, no earth, no minds, no bodies; was I not then likewise persuaded that I did not exist? On the contrary, if I persuaded myself of something, then I certainly existed. But there is some deceiver, supremely powerful and supremely intelligent, who purposely always deceives me. Then undoubtedly I exist if he deceives me; let him deceive me as much as he can, he will never bring it about that I am nothing while I am thinking that I am something. So that, having weighed all considerations enough and more than enough, I must at length con-

clude that this proposition "I am", "I exist" is necessarily true whenever I utter it or conceive it in my
mind. (AT VII, 25; HR I, 150)

In this passage, having first remarked that it does
not clearly follow from the nonexistence of his body
that he does not himself exist, Descartes proceeds to
prove his existence from several alternative premises.
Instead of the single *cogito*, we have four arguments
suggested.

(1) I persuaded myself there was nothing . . .
    so I existed.
(2) An omnipotent deceiver deceives me . . . so
    I exist.
(3) I think that I am something . . . so I am
    not nothing.
(4) I conceive the proposition "I am" . . . so
    "I am" is true.

The first argument is a past-tense version of the *cogito*,
with "I persuaded myself that there was nothing" as
the premise recording a particular thought. The second
shows that the *cogito* is invulnerable even to the hypothesis of the evil genius. It differs from the normal
cogito in two ways: It has a hypothetical, not an indubitable, premise ("if he deceives me . . ."), and it
argues to the existence of the self as the object of deception, not as the subject of thought ("me" must stand
for something). In the third argument, again we have
a particular version of the *cogito*, with "I think that I
am something" as its premise; the conclusion points
forward to the further conclusion "I am not deceived in
thinking that I am something." This further connection

is made explicit in the fourth argument. Here the premise is not "I think that I am" but "I think of the proposition 'I am,' " and the conclusion is not the simple "I exist" but " 'I exist' is true." Whenever Descartes thinks, he can prove his existence; so whenever he has the thought "I exist" he can prove that the thought is true. Consequently, the thought is not only true but certain —he can never at any time have reason to doubt it—for he cannot even consider whether to doubt it without thinking of it, and he cannot think of it without its being true.

Such, then, is the structure of the *cogito*. What of its validity? Arguments may be brought against the premise, against the inference, and against the conclusion. We shall consider each in turn.

Many people, from Leibniz onward, have objected to the presence of the word "I" in the premise "I am thinking." Russell may serve as an example. "The word 'I' is really illegitimate," he wrote, "[for] he ought to state his ultimate premise in the form 'there are thoughts'. The word 'I' is grammatically convenient, but does not describe a datum." [10] Of course, it doesn't, Descartes might reply; it refers to something inferred. In the *Second Meditation*, just after the *cogito*, he says, "I do not yet understand what is this 'I' that necessarily exists. I must take care, then, that I do not rashly take something else for the 'I', and thus go wrong even in the knowledge that I am maintaining to be the most certain and evident of all." What "I" stands for is doubtful, even after the *cogito*; what "think" refers to has to be unmistakable before the *cogito* can start. Descartes cannot, therefore, be taking it as a datum that the "I" in "I am thinking" has a reference, as Russell maintains.

A more sophisticated objection to the "I" in the "*cogito*" has been made recently by Peter Geach.[11] Geach says that Descartes implies that "introspection can give the word 'I' a special sense, which each of us can learn on his own account"; when a speaker uses "I" he refers not to the man whom others can see, but to something distinct, which is discernible by an inward gaze. This, Geach says, is mistaken. "I" is used in ordinary life to draw people's attention to the speaker. When it is used by Descartes in soliloquy, however, it does not serve to direct Descartes' attention to himself or to show that it is Descartes and none other who is engaged in meditation. "We are not to argue, though, that since 'I' does not refer to the man René Descartes it has some other, more intangible, thing to refer to. Rather, in this context the word 'I' is idle, superfluous." Someone who looks for something other than the human being who speaks to be the reference of the soliloquist's "I" is falling into the ancient trap of thinking that every word must stand for something.

It does not seem to me that Descartes here fell into this trap. He would, I think, have agreed with Geach that "in soliloquy he could quite well have expressed himself without using the first-person pronoun at all; he could have said 'This is really a dreadful muddle', where 'this' would refer back to his previous meditations." In stating the conclusion of the *cogito* Descartes several times stresses the first person by adding a pronoun, "*ego*," which is superfluous in Latin. He does not similarly stress the first person in the premise of the *cogito*.

He does not need to. When he thinks, he is aware of a thought—no matter, yet, to whom or what the thought belongs. Since, by the light of nature, he knows what a thought is, he knows that it is an attribute and not a substance. Again, by the light of nature, he knows that every such attribute must belong to a substance. So he concludes to the existence of the substance of which the thought he perceives is an attribute. This he calls *ego*; or, if you like, he concludes that the "I" in "I am thinking" does refer to a substance and is not just a grammatical convenience. (Thus, for example, he sometimes expresses his conclusion in the form "I am something" [AT VII, 24, l. 25].) This line of thought is particularly clear in the *Principles,* where Descartes is explaining how we can know our soul more clearly than our body.

> It is very manifest by the natural light which is in our souls, that no qualities or properties pertain to nothing; and that where some are perceived there must necessarily be some thing or substance on which they depend. And the same light shows us that we know a thing or substance so much the better the more properties we observe in it. And we certainly observe many more qualities in our mind than in any other thing.

He then goes on to say that everything we know involves a piece of conscious thinking, and each such episode is a "quality or property" through which we come to know the substance that is our thinking soul or self (AT VIII, 9; HR I, 223).

A different objection might be made to the premise "*cogito.*" Is it really indubitable? Even if I do not really

see a light, Descartes argued, at least I seem to see a
light, I think I see a light; and this cannot be doubted.
But might not the evil genius be deceiving him into
thinking that he seems to see a light when in fact he
seems to smell a rose? Descartes never really faced up to
this objection. Of course, it might be argued that even if
I only think I think I see a light, still it remains true that
I *think*. But Descartes did not give this reply; and he
seems to have disabled himself from doing so when he
told Hobbes that it was absurd to talk of one thought's
being the topic of another thought (AT VII, 175; HR
II, 64).

What of the "*ergo*" in the *cogito*? Hintikka argued
that, considered as an inference, the passage from
thought to existence was invalid; Hamlet thought, but
Hamlet did not exist. To this, it seems to me, one might
well reply that in just the same sense as "Hamlet existed" is false, "Hamlet thought" is also false. Hamlet's
thoughts are no less and no more imaginary than Hamlet's existence. It is possible to give many different
philosophical accounts of the status of fictional characters; but on no coherent interpretation does "Hamlet
thought, therefore Hamlet existed" have a true premise
and a false conclusion. The reason we cannot use the
cogito to prove Hamlet's existence is that no one can be
aware of Hamlet's thoughts in the way in which Descartes was aware of his own thoughts.

Nonetheless, the principle that where there are
attributes there must be a substance does not seem as
unquestionable since the writings of Berkeley and Hume
as it did to Descartes. Too often, when Descartes tells
us that something is taught by the natural light in our

souls, he produces a doctrine taught by the Jesuits at La Flèche. And, as we shall see in Chapter Seven, this particular principle—that what has attributes must exist —appears to be rejected by Descartes himself in his presentation of the ontological argument.

But even if we accept the principle, there seems some doubt whether the conclusion it licenses is in fact "*sum*." Is not Descartes rash in christening the substance in which the doubts of the *Meditations* inhere "*ego*"? To be sure, he explains that he is not yet committing himself to any doctrine about the nature of the *ego*; not until the *Sixth Meditation*, for instance, will he prove that it is incorporeal. But what "I" refers to must at least be distinct from what "you" refers to; otherwise the argument might as well run "*cogitatur, ergo es*" as "*cogito ergo sum*." Has Descartes any right to make such an assumption about the substance in which these thoughts inhere? In 1641 Hyperaspistes wrote: "You do not know whether it is you yourself who think, or whether the world-soul in you thinks, as the Platonists believe" (AT III, 404). To this pertinent criticism Descartes had no real reply.

FOUR

SUM
RES
COGITANS

I

The *cogito* provided Descartes with three things. First, it established as certain his own existence. This we have considered in the previous chapter.

Second, it suggested to him a general criterion for truth and certainty.

> Observing that there is nothing at all in the statement "I am thinking, therefore I exist" which assures me that I speak the truth, except that I see very clearly that in order to think I must exist, I judged that I could take it as a general rule that whatever we conceive very clearly and very distinctly is true.

This we shall consider in Chapter Eight.

Third, it enabled Descartes to discover his own

nature. I think, therefore I am. But what am I? A thinking thing. The present chapter will examine the relation between *cogito ergo sum* and *sum res cogitans*.

In the *Discourse*, Descartes argued thus:

> I next considered attentively what I was; and I saw that while I could pretend that I had no body, that there was no world, and no place for me to be in, I could not pretend that I was not; on the contrary, from the mere fact that I thought of doubting the truth of other things it evidently and certainly followed that I existed. On the other hand, if I had merely ceased to think, even if everything else that I had ever imagined had been true, I had no reason to believe that I should have existed. From this I recognized that I was a substance whose whole essence or nature is to think and whose being requires no place and depends on no material thing. (AT VI, 33; HR I, 101)

In the *Second Meditation*, having decided that "I exist" is true whenever uttered or thought, Descartes adds: "But I do not yet know clearly enough what I am, I who am certain that I am, and hence I must be careful to see that I do not imprudently mistake some other object for myself." The pruning process of Cartesian doubt, which has stripped him of all his beliefs about the world save one, is now to be applied to the content of this belief. The result is that "I do not observe that any other thing necessarily pertains to my nature or essence, save that I am a thinking thing" (AT VII, 78; HR I, 190).

Before examining the arguments Descartes offers, we must investigate the content of the conclusion that he is a thing whose essence it is to think. The terminology of essence is scholastic, and so, despite disclaimers elsewhere, is the whole method of procedure. Existence, said the scholastics, is what corresponds to the question *an sit?* asked of an entity; essence is what one describes in answering the question *quid sit?* Just as Aquinas, in the *Summa Theologiae*, having proved the existence of God, goes on to discuss the nature of God, so Descartes, having proved his own existence, goes on to inquire about his essence, asking what kind of thing he may be.

"Thing" (*res*) is used by Descartes as a synonym for "substance" (*substantia*). By "substance" the scholastics meant a concrete entity, such as water, or a dog, or an angel, as opposed to an abstraction such as humanity or sadness or yesterday. The essence of a substance was given by the answer to the question "What kind of thing is it?" To find the essence you had to look for those predicates that must be true of a thing if it was to exist at all as the kind of thing it was. Thus, to be an animal was part of the essence of a dog, because nothing could ever be a dog without being an animal. But to be black or to be barking did not belong to the essence of a dog, because not all dogs were black and no dog was always barking.

Descartes took over the scholastic notion of substance. "Everything in which there resides immediately, as in a subject, or by means of which there exists anything that we perceive, i.e. any property, quality or attribute, of which we have a real idea, is called a Substance" (AT VII, 161; HR II, 53). "By Substance," he said in the *Principles*, "we can understand nothing else than a thing which so exists that it needs no other thing in order to exist." He observed that, strictly speaking, only God was a substance so defined, but created substances could be said to be "things which need only the concurrence of God in order to exist" (AT VIII, 24; HR I, 240). According to the scholastics, there were many different kinds of substances. For Descartes, there were only two: mind, or thinking substance; and body, or extended substance. The essence of mind was thought; the essence of body was extension.

A thing is not to be identified with its essence. When Descartes says that his essence is thinking, he does not mean that he can use "I" and "thought" as synonyms. The essence of a substance is something that substance *has*. "Besides the attribute which specifies a substance," he told Burman, "we must recognize the substance itself beneath the attribute; for instance, the soul, being a thinking thing, is, in addition to thought, a substance which thinks" (AT V, 156). Substances, Descartes says, have modes and attributes; we might say variable and invariable properties. Among the attributes of a substance is its essence. "There is always one principal attribute of a substance which constitutes its nature and essence, and on which all the others depend" (AT VIII, 25; HR I, 240). "We must distinguish between those things, which of their nature can change, as that I am now writing or am not writing, that one man is wise and another unwise; and those things which never change, as are all those things that belong to the essence of a thing" (AT VIII, 2a, 347; HR I, 435).

Descartes made clear in his controversy with Hobbes that when he said his essence was thinking he did not mean that he was identical either with thought in the abstract or with his own faculty of thinking (AT VII, 174; HR II, 62–63). In the *Principles*, however, there is a puzzling passage: "We may consider thought and extension as constituting the natures of intelligent and corporeal substance; and then they must not be considered otherwise than as the very substances that think and are extended, i.e. as mind and body" (AT VIII, 31; HR I, 245). This passage has led scholars to think that Descartes identified mind with thought. But what Descartes says is that thought constitutes the *nature* of intelligent substance, and the nature of a substance is not the substance itself. Some light is cast on this by another passage from the *Interview with Burman*. "All the attributes taken together are in truth the same thing as a substance; but not the attributes taken singly apart from the others" (AT V, 154). This is true even of the principal attribute that constitutes the nature.

The contrast that Descartes is concerned to make in the *Principles* is not that between a substance and its faculties, but between a faculty and its particular thoughts. Thought is the essence of mind in the sense that each mind must always be thinking some thought or other, but particular thoughts come and go and none of them is essential.

We may likewise consider thoughts and extension as modes which are found in substance; that is, in as far as we consider that one and the same mind may have many different thoughts, and that one body, retaining the same size, may be extended in many different ways, sometimes being greater in length and less in breadth or depth, and sometimes on the contrary greater in breadth and less in length. (AT VIII, 31; HR I, 246)

Descartes makes this clearer in a letter to Arnauld in 1648.

I tried to remove ambiguity from the word *thought* in the articles 63 and 64 of the first part of my *Principles*. Just as extension, which constitutes the nature of body, differs greatly from the various shapes or modes which it takes on; so thought, or thinking nature, which I consider constitutes the essence of the human mind, is far from being this or that act of thinking. Mind has from itself the power of choosing this or that act of thought, but not that of being a thinking substance, just as a flame has of itself, in its capacity as efficient cause, the power of extending itself on one side or the other, but not that of being an extended thing. By thought, therefore, I understand not a universal comprehending all the modes of thinking, but a particular nature which receives all the modes just as extension is a nature which receives all the shapes. (AT V, 221; cf. Letter to Mesland, AT V, 114)[1]

It is time to examine more closely what Descartes meant by "think," or rather by the verbs *"cogitare"* and *"penser."* As was said in Chapter Three, he used the verbs to record many mental events that we would not naturally describe as thoughts. It has been said that the words in the current French and Latin of Descartes' time had a sense wider than that of the modern English equivalent; that may be so.[2] However, French and Latin usage was never as wide as that found in Descartes; at no time was it natural to call a headache or a pang of hunger a *cogitatio* or *pensée*. In fact, Descartes was consciously extending the use of the words "*cogitare*" and "*penser*." This is brought out by the misunderstandings of his contemporaries. Mersenne, for example, objected that if the nature of man consisted solely of thought, then man has no will. "I do not see that this follows," Descartes had to explain, "for willing, understanding, imagining and feeling are simply different modes of thinking, which all belong to the soul" (Letter to Mersenne, AT I, 366). To another correspondent Descartes wrote in 1638:

> There is nothing entirely in our power except our thoughts; at least if you take the word "thought" as I do, for all the operations of the soul, in such a way that not only meditations and acts of the will, but even the functions of sight and hearing, and the resolving on one movement rather than another, in so far as they depend on the soul, are all thoughts. (AT II, 36)

I have used the traditional translation "thought" for "*pensée*" and "*cogitatio*." The English word seems unnatural in some contexts, but not more unnatural than the corresponding words seemed in similar contexts to Descartes' contemporaries.

Descartes gives various lists of particular kinds of thought. He mentions doubting, understanding, affirming, denying, being willing or unwilling, imagining, and all forms of sense perception (AT VII, 28; HR I, 153; AT VII, 160; HR II, 54; AT VIII, 7; HR I, 222). He frequently calls these *modi cogitandi*. This expression is quite naturally translated "ways of thinking," but it can also be taken to be a use of Descartes' technical sense of "mode." Particular thoughts are variable properties of the substance that is mind. A mind must always be thinking; but it need not always be judging or willing or imagining. Thought is "the principal property of (mental) substance which constitutes its nature and essence and on which all the others depend" (AT VIII, 25; HR I, 240). We can think without perceiving, but we cannot perceive without thinking; and so for all the other modes of thought. All the modes, however, are to be related to two general modes: perception (the operation of the intellect) and volition (the operation of the will). Sense perception, imagination, and pure understanding are modes of perceiving, while desire, aversion, affirmation, denial, and doubt are modes of willing (AT VIII, 17; HR I, 232).[3]

Descartes extended the concept of thought in this manner because of a feature he believed to attach to all the operations of the soul. "By the noun 'thought,' " he wrote in the *Principles*, "I mean everything which takes place in us so that we are conscious of it (*nobis consciis*), in so far as it is an object of consciousness" (AT VIII, 7; HR I, 222). In the *Second Replies* he defined thought as what is in us in such a way that we are *immediately* conscious of it. "I added 'immediately,' " he explained, "for the purpose of excluding the consequences of thoughts; voluntary movements, for instance, depend upon thoughts but are not themselves thoughts" (AT VII, 160; HR II, 54).

What is common to all the operations of the mind is consciousness. Consciousness carries with it indubitability and thus makes the *cogito* suitable as a first prin-

ciple. Sensation, as well as intellectual thought, is a
thought capable of assuring the certainty of one's own
existence. But does not sensation presuppose a body?
How then can its occurrence be certain while the existence of body is doubtful? (AT VII, 27; HR I, 150.)
Descartes explains that there are two different ways of
taking "sensation." The sentence "I see" may be used
to refer to a corporeal action, in which case its truth is
not indubitable; in sleep I may think I am seeing though
I do not open my eyes. "But if I take it to refer to the
actual sensation or consciousness of seeing . . . then
it is quite certain; for in that case it has regard to the
mind, and it is the mind alone that has a sense or
thought of itself seeing (*sentit sive cogitat se videre*)"
(AT VIII, 7; HR I, **222**). Sensation so understood, Descartes says, is thought (AT VII, 29; HR I, 153).

In thus identifying sensation with thought, Descartes is perhaps not so much extending the scope of
cogitatio as altering that of *sensus*. If Macbeth says he
sees a dagger where no dagger is, we may hesitate to
say whether he sees anything at all; but it is perfectly
natural to say he *thinks* he sees a dagger. Now this same
thought, on Descartes' view, occurs also when Macbeth
really is, in the normal sense, seeing a dagger; it is
thought of this kind in which sensation strictly so called
consists and that provides a premise for the *cogito*.
Such thoughts can be mistaken, but their occurrence
and content cannot be doubted.

It is I who have sensations, or who perceive corporeal
objects as it were by the senses. Thus, I am now
seeing light, hearing a noise, feeling heat. These
objects are unreal, for I am asleep; but at least I seem

to see, to hear, to be warmed. This cannot be unreal, and this is what is properly called my sensation; further sensation, precisely so regarded, is nothing but an act of [thought]. (AT VII, 29; HR I, 153)

In one respect the Macbeth example is misleading. It *seemed to* Macbeth that he was seeing a dagger; but he did not *think* he was seeing a dagger unless he *believed* there was a dagger there. In expounding Descartes, however, it would be wrong to identify the thought that one is seeing with the belief or judgment that one is seeing in the ordinary sense of "see." The thought that one is seeing is an act of the intellect; the judgment is an act of the will. The occurrence of the belief is not a necessary condition for the occurrence of the corresponding thought. During his period of doubt Descartes has the thought that he is seeing a light—that is, it seems to him that he is seeing a light—but he refrains from believing this. Again, the occurrence of a belief is not a sufficient condition for the occurrence of the corresponding thought. The intellectual perception that a limb has been hurt is not the same as the feeling of pain in that limb (AT VII, 82; HR I, 192).

It seems that to have the thought that p is to have an experience similar to the experience I have when I would normally say that p is the case. The occurrence of thoughts is not open to doubt or error. Thoughts cannot occur without our knowing that they occur, and we cannot think that a thought is occurring unless that thought actually is occurring. Perhaps I only think I see; but that I think I see cannot be doubted. Note that it is not just the occurrence of *thought* that cannot be doubted, but the occurrence of the particular thought in question (AT VII, 29).

It is difficult to give an account of Descartes' theory without unnaturalness. Comparison of the various texts makes it clear that what is referred to by "think" in "thinking I am seeing" and by "seem" in "seeming to hear" is to be identified with the consciousness or perception by which Descartes defines the nature of *cogitatio*, or thought. (In the *Principles*, for instance, when Descartes is explaining how any conscious activity is capable of providing a premise for the *cogito*, he uses "*putare me videre*" in parallel with "*conscientia videndi*" and with "*mens cogitat se videre*.") But we cannot say that the consciousness, or perception, or awareness of sensation may occur whether or not sensation occurs; "to be conscious of," "to perceive," and "to be aware of" seem to be used in such a way that one can only be conscious of, perceive, and be aware of what is really the case. They are what Gilbert Ryle has called "success verbs." [4] On the other hand, it is odd to say that "seeming to see" or "thinking that one sees" may occur whether or not seeing occurs; "seeming to see" and "thinking that one sees" seem to be phrases designed to cover just the case in which one *does not* see. The *cogitatio* of seeing is meant to be what is common to the genuine case and the doubtful case. Descartes would indeed be contemptuous of any "ordinary-language" argument against the coherence of the notion of *cogitatio*. "A man," he said, "who makes it his aim to raise his knowledge above the common should be ashamed to derive the occasion for doubting from the forms of speech invented by the vulgar" (AT VII, 32;

HR I, 156). We shall see later, however, that it is not just an accident of idiom that there is no natural way of referring to an element common to veridical and deceptive sense perception.

Certainly in Descartes' theory there is an ambiguity. Sometimes consciousness appears to be something that accompanies thought, as when he says that thought is that *of which* we are conscious (*Second Replies*, AT VII, 160; HR II, 52). Sometimes consciousness appears to be something identical with thought, as when he says that it is our seeming to see that is strictly to be called sensation or thought (*Second Meditation*, AT VII, 29; HR I, 153). And in passages in which thought and consciousness are identified, it is often unclear whether particular mental acts are species of thought consciousness or are accompanied by thought consciousness (cf. AT VII, 176 and AT IX, 137).[5]

The difficulty arises naturally from the way in which *cogitatio* is introduced. Sensation in the non-Cartesian sense is a conscious act in the sense that it is itself a mode of consciousness; to see a sphere and to feel a sphere are two different ways of being conscious of the sphere. But willing is not a conscious act in the same way; to want to be certain is not to be conscious of being certain. Wanting can only be claimed to be a conscious act in the different sense that if I want something, I am conscious that I want it. Wanting is not a mode of consciousness, but may be accompanied by consciousness. Sensation, too, is accompanied by consciousness; if I perceive something, then I am conscious that I perceive it. But sensation and willing differ. Willing is conscious only in the sense of being an object of consciousness; sensation is conscious not only in this sense, but also in the sense of being a mode of consciousness.

This difference between willing and sensation is preserved in the Cartesian system, but transposed onto a different plane. Since sensation, strictly so called, is nothing more than the seeming to perceive something, it cannot be defined as a mode of consciousness of anything extramental. But even Cartesian sensations are perceptions *as it were* of external objects. Descartes says that they differ from volitions and feelings in that "we refer them to objects outside which strike our senses" (AT XI, 35; HR I, 342). Sensations and volitions are alike, however, in that they are "things in us of which we are immediately conscious." And so the question arises whether the relation between them and this immediate consciousness is one of concomitance or identity.

In the case of willing, Descartes gives an explicit answer. "It is certain that we cannot desire anything without perceiving by the same means that we desire it . . . this perception and this desire are really one and the same thing" (HR II, 341). This answer seems incorrect. A perception and a desire are altogether different things: a perception, in this sense, is the possession of a piece of information that may be characterized as true or false; a desire is an attitude that may be good or evil but cannot be called true or false. Perhaps Descartes means not that the perception and the desire are identical, but that they cannot occur without each other. This seems open to question. Each of us has desires that he does not recognize, and we often believe ourselves to desire things about which in fact we do not care. Such desires, however, would have to be long-term dispositions; and Descartes is thinking of particular mental episodes.

What answer would Descartes give to the parallel question: What is the relation between seeming to see and being aware that I seem to see? Hobbes said, "It is not by another thought that I recognize that I think . . . This would lead to an endless series of questions: how do you know that you know that you know?" (AT VII, 173; HR II, 62.) Descartes' reply was that no one but Hobbes had ever imagined that one thought could be the topic of another thought. Unless he had missed the point of the objection, he must have meant that a thought such as seeming to see was identical with the awareness of seeming to see. But if this is so, then the consciousness of a thought is no different from the thought itself and cannot be used by Descartes as the mark that distinguishes cogitative activities of human beings from their corporeal activities. In fact, of course, a man's seeing an object is distinguished from his kicking an object because seeing, unlike kicking, is a way of being conscious of the object. But as we have seen, Descartes cannot appeal to consciousness in *this* sense as a distinguishing mark of *cogitationes*. Nor can he appeal to the fact that sensation involves "referring perceptions to objects outside." This cannot be the characteristic mark of thoughts, since there are some thoughts, for instance volitions, that lack this feature.

Hobbes seems to have laid his finger on the feature that makes the notion of Cartesian consciousness incoherent. If *conscientia* adds nothing to a mental event, then it cannot be used to distinguish mental events from physical ones. If it adds to a mental event something extra, then we must consider the possibility that this extra element might be present without the appropriate mental event's being present. In that case, my having the awareness that I seem to see will be no guarantee that I do in fact seem to see; Hobbes can start his vicious regress and there will be no quietus for Cartesian doubt.

If the awareness of a thought adds anything to the thought itself, it seems that it must include at least a correct identification of the thought. And if it is to be possible to correctly identify a thought, it seems that we must be able to distinguish between what makes an identification the particular identification it is, and what makes it a correct identification. For instance, if I correctly identify a particular thought as a pain, there must be some feature of what I do that makes it an identification *as pain*, and there must be some different circumstance that makes it a *correct* identification. If the two elements were the same—if the content of my identification were specified by the very same element that makes it a correct identification—then it would be idle to distinguish between correct and incorrect identification at all.

An example may make this clearer. If I say of an adult human that he is conscious that he is in pain, I may mean more than that he is in pain. I may mean that he can *say* he is in pain. If a man can say that he is in pain, he can say falsely that he is in pain. But if this is to be possible, that which gives his utterance "I am in pain" its meaning must be something other than that which gives it its truth, namely, his being in pain. In this case, a man who said truthfully, "I am in pain," could perhaps be said to be correctly identifying his sensation as a pain. But this can only mean that he understands correctly how to use the word "pain"; and this understanding cannot be what makes the difference between the truthful and mendacious utterance of "I'm in pain." That difference is made simply by the presence or absence of pain itself.

The criticism I am making of Cartesian consciousness was suggested by a famous argument of Ludwig Wittgenstein to show the impossibility of a private language.[6] But the criticism does not depend on any thesis about the nature of language. The utterance "I am in pain" was considered merely as a possible way in which a man might be said to show awareness of his sensations. The criticism is based on a quite general principle. What makes my awareness an awareness *of pain* cannot simply be the fact that it occurs in conjunction with pain. For the presence of pain is what gives my awareness its truth, not its content. What, then, makes it an awareness of pain at all? Descartes suggests no answer, and it is hard to see what answer he could suggest. If there is no answer, then his concept of consciousness seems doubly faulty. Not only has he no reply to Hobbes' question, "How do you know that your belief that you have a certain thought is true?"; he has no reply either to Wittgenstein's question, "How do you even know what is the content of that belief?"

II

Having analyzed the meaning of Descartes' claim that his essence is thinking, we may now return to the proof he offers in support of his claim. In *The Search After Truth* Polyander announces that he is certain that he exists and that he is not a body "otherwise, doubting of my body I should at the same time doubt of myself, and this I cannot do; for I am absolutely convinced that I exist" (AT X, 518; HR I, 319). This appears to offer an argument that is suggested by several passages in Descartes' writings, notably the one from the *Discourse* cited at the beginning of this chapter (AT VIII, 7; HR I, 221). The argument runs thus:

(1) My body can be feigned by me not to exist.

(2) I cannot be feigned by me not to exist.

Ergo (3) My body is not the same as I.

This argument is of the form: Fa not Fb; *ergo* $a \neq b$. It must depend on the principle that if two things are identical, then whatever is true of one is true of the other—a principle sometimes nicknamed "the principle of the indiscernibility of identicals." [7] From this principle it follows that if something is true of a but not true of b, then a is not identical with b. The principle, so far as I know, is not enunciated by Descartes, but it might well seem obvious enough to be something known by natural light. Nonetheless, the principle has been questioned by philosophers. In particular it has been denied that the principle applies in modal contexts (those involving the notions of necessity and possibility) and in intentional contexts (those involving notions such as belief and desire). The principle seems to admit of exceptions in modal contexts: Four is the number of the Gospels, and it is necessarily true that four is twice two; but it is not necessarily true that the number of the Gospels is twice two—it is merely contingently true. The principle seems to admit of exceptions in intentional contexts: Dr. Jekyll is identical with Mr. Hyde, yet Dr. Jekyll may be believed to be a good man without Mr. Hyde being believed to be a good man. But the predicate ". . . can be feigned by me not to exist" provides a context that is both modal and intentional, since it concerns the *possibility* of a certain *pretense*. Therefore, we cannot assume without argument that the principle of the indiscernibility of identicals holds in this case. Indeed, it seems clear that it does not. Ferdinand in *The Tempest* is in doubt whether his father has been shipwrecked and whether he himself has thereby succeeded to the throne of Naples. He cannot settle this doubt by arguing, "I can doubt whether the King of Naples exists (I can imagine Naples having become a republic); but I cannot doubt whether I exist; therefore I am not the King of Naples." Yet this seems parallel to the argument set out above.

The passage from the *Discourse* concludes not only that Descartes is not identical with his body, but also that he does not depend for his existence on his body or any material thing. This is a stronger conclusion; for it would be possible for him to be dependent on his body without being identified with his body. This would be so, for instance, if his body were an indispensable *part* of himself. He observes that the proof of his existence depends upon his thinking, but does not depend upon the existence of his body or of the world. He concludes that his existence depends upon his thinking, and that his existence does not depend upon the existence of his body or of the world. This makes it look as if he is using some general principle to the effect that the existence of A depends upon B if, and only if, the proof of the existence of A depends upon B. But this is not a principle he can accept, for he later gives a proof of the existence of God that depends upon the existence of his idea of God. But he would not wish to say that the existence of God depended upon the existence of his idea of God. For God might exist without any creature existing.

However, the argument in the *Discourse* suggests a different interpretation. Consider the following five propositions:

(4) I am thinking.
(5) I have a body.
(6) I am in a world.
(7) I am in a place.
(8) I exist.

Descartes draws our attention to the following facts about these propositions and their relations to each other. First, (5), (6), and (7) are uncertain, while (8) is certain ("I could feign that I had no body, that there was no world, and no place existed for me to be in; I could not feign that I was not"). If (4) is true, and (5),

(6), and (7) are doubtful, (8) is certain ("From the mere fact that I thought of doubting about other truths, it evidently and certainly followed that I existed"). If (4) is false, and (5), (6), and (7) are true, (8) is not certain ("If I had merely ceased from thinking, even if everything else that I had ever imagined had been true, I had no reason to believe that I should still have existed").

From all this it follows that (4) is a premise whose truth is both necessary and sufficient to establish the certainty of (8); whereas (5), (6), and (7) are premises none of which is necessary, and which together are insufficient, to establish the certainty of (8). It is true, of course, and indeed certain, that each of the propositions (4)–(7) entails the proposition (8). But for a premise to establish a conclusion as certain, it is not sufficient that it should certainly entail the conclusion; it is necessary also that it should itself be certain. Now (5), (6), and (7) are not necessary to establish the certainty of (8), because even if each of them is doubtful, the certainty of (8) can be derived from the truth of (4). Moreover, the truth of (5), (6), and (7) is not sufficient to establish the certainty of (8), not because (5), (6), and (7) do not entail (8), but because even if true they are doubtful. The truth of (4) on the other hand is necessary to establish the certainty of (8). This, I take it, is what Descartes means when he says, ". . . from the mere fact that I thought . . . it evidently and certainly followed that I existed." The "evidently" refers to the self-evidence of the entailment of "I exist" by "I think"; the "certainly" means that if "I think" is true, then "I exist" is certain. For this to be the case, "I am thinking" must be certain whenever it is true. This is not said here by Descartes; but it accords with his general theory.

The conclusion is drawn that my existence depends only on my thinking ("I am a being whose *whole* essence or nature is to think") and rests not at all on the existence of any body, place, or world ("and whose being requires no place or no material thing"). Clearly, some step has been omitted. Can we fill it in?

One principle that would enable Descartes to derive his conclusion from his premises might run as follows. Those properties constitute the essence of a thing that are severally necessary and jointly sufficient to establish the existence of that thing with certainty. This principle, coupled with the premise that the single property of thinking is both necessary and sufficient to establish with certainty my own existence, will yield the conclusion that my essence is constituted by thinking.

Two considerations make this principle plausible. First, it seems reasonable to say that those properties constitute the essence of a thing that are severally necessary and jointly sufficient for the thing to exist. Second, if the holding of a given property makes "I exist" certain, then *a fortiori* it seems to establish it as true.

These considerations notwithstanding, the principle is in fact false, as is easily shown. For let us suppose that it is true, but not indubitable, that it is impossible to think without having a body. Then all Descartes' premises will remain true. Proposition (4) alone will be necessary and sufficient to establish the certainty of (8); for (5), though it follows from (4) in conjunction with the hypothesis that it is impossible to think without having a body, is not certain since that hypothesis is itself doubtful. But Descartes' conclusion will be false. For if it is in fact impossible to think without having a body, then it cannot be true both that my essence is thinking and that my existence does not depend at all on the existence of any body. The suggested principle, therefore, since it would permit the drawing of a false conclusion from true premises, must be rejected.

It is not clear whether Descartes is appealing to such a principle. When the *Discourse* was published, critics objected that

> . . . it does not follow from the fact that the human mind reflecting on itself does not perceive itself to be other than a thing that thinks, that its nature or its essence consists only in its being a thing that thinks, in the sense that this word *only* excludes all other things which might also be supposed to pertain to the nature of the soul. (AT VII, 8; HR I, 137)

To this objection Descartes replied in the Preface to the *Meditations*

> . . . it was not my intention in that place to exclude these in accordance with the order that looks to the truth of the matter (as to which I was not then dealing), but only in accordance with the order of my thought; thus my meaning was that so far as I was aware, I knew nothing clearly as belonging to my essence, excepting that I was a thing that thinks. (AT VII, 8; HR I, 137)

Norman Malcolm[8] has pointed out that in this passage Descartes misrepresents his argument in the *Discourse*, which concluded not that thinking was the only clearly known element in his essence, but that he was a substance whose *whole* essence or nature was to think. But in the *Meditations* Descartes does proceed more circumspectly.

Having established the certainty of "I exist," he asks himself what the "I" in this sentence stands for. What is the subject whose existence is revealed by the perception of the attribute of thought? He decides, without proof, that the "I" defined as "the substance in which this thought inheres" will be the same as whatever resists Cartesian doubt in the plain man's concept of "I." Hitherto, he thought of himself as a being with a body that was nourished, that moved, and that had sensations and thoughts. But until the hypothesis of the evil genius is exorcised, he cannot be sure that he has a body, or that he moves or is nourished, or that he has sensations insofar as these depend on sense organs. The only property he hitherto believed himself to possess that cannot be rendered doubtful by his hyperbolical hypothesis is thought.

> There is thought: of this and this only I cannot be deprived. I am, I exist; that is certain. For how long? For as long as I am thinking; maybe if I wholly ceased to think, I should at once wholly cease to be. For the present I am admitting only what is necessarily true; I am, with this qualification, no more than a conscious being (*sum igitur praecise tantum res cogitans*). (AT VII, 27; HR I, 152)

In this passage, it is clear, by "necessarily true" Descartes does not mean anything equivalent to "logically true," but rather what is certain, what resists Cartesian doubt. When he says, "I am, with this qualification, no more than a thinking being," he means "I am, qua known for certain, no more than a conscious being." We may compare *The Search After Truth,* where Eudoxus says to Polyander, "Tell me what you are *inasmuch as you doubt*" (AT X, 517; HR I, 318).

Descartes offers two proofs of this. First, all the properties I have hitherto ascribed to myself are vulnerable to Cartesian doubt, except that of thinking. Second, "I exist," the conclusion of the *cogito,* is certain when and only when I am thinking. So I, qua known for certain, exist when and only when I am thinking. In this sense, I, qua known for certain, am no more than a thinking being. Whether, therefore, we start from the I that is referred to by ordinary language or from the I that is the subject whose existence is established by the *cogito,* we reach the conclusion that I, qua known for certain, am no more than a thinking being.

The way in which Descartes expresses himself lays a number of traps. First, it is easy to confuse the following two propositions:

(9) I am not known for certain to have any property other than thought.
(10) I am known for certain to have no property other than thought.

Of these two propositions, (9) is clear but (10) is ambiguous. It may be understood as equivalent to (9) or as equivalent to:

(11) It is known for certain that I have no property other than thought.

Second, one can be led into thinking that "I, qua known for certain" designates a subject of predication in the same way as "I," so that I,-qua-known-for-certain would be perhaps a core or element of the plain I, with properties of its own.

In the next passage we can see Descartes picking his way through these traps.

> I am a thinking being. And what more? I shall use my imagination. I am not that collection of members which we call the human body: I am not a subtle air infused into these members, I am not a wind, a fire, a vapour, a breath, nor anything at all which I can imagine; because I have supposed that all these things do not exist. (AT VII, 27; HR I, 152)

Here it looks at first as if we had the fallacious argument from the indiscernibility of identicals considered above. (Body is being supposed not to exist; I am not being supposed not to exist; so I am not identical with body.) But in fact, what is being asserted is that I, *qua known for certain*, am not any bodily entity. To establish this conclusion, the argument seems persuasive enough. For if I know for certain that I am identical with a body, then I cannot consistently suppose all bodies not to exist without supposing myself not to exist. The next passage makes it clear that Descartes has this weaker conclusion in mind.

> Perhaps it is the case that these very things which I suppose non-existent, because they are unknown to me, are yet not different in reality from the I which I know (*ab eo me quem novi*). I do not know, and will not now dispute the point; I can judge only of what I know. I know that I exist, and I want to

discover what is this I which I know (*quis sim ego ille quem novi*). Assuredly, the knowledge of this I so qualified (*huius sic praecise sumpti notitiam*) does not depend on those things whose existence I do not yet know; and therefore not on what I feign in imagination. (AT VII, 28; HR I, 152)

Notice the complications into which Descartes' logical syntax leads him. "*Ego quem novi*" is ambiguous. It may mean "I, who am known by me," or "I, qua known by me." The first time it is used in this passage it must be taken in the former sense: the I, who is known by me to be a *res cogitans*, may also be, for all I know, a body. The second time it is used it must be taken in the latter sense. The I, qua known by me to be a *res cogitans*, is no more than that. "I, qua known by me am only a *res cogitans*" is a dangerous formulation, because it is ambiguous between "I only know that I am a thinking thing" and "I know that I am only a thinking thing." Was Descartes tricked by this ambiguity?

In reply to critics in his lifetime, Descartes always drew attention to the passage just quoted and insisted that in the *Second Meditation* he did not assert that there was nothing corporeal in the soul, but only that nothing corporeal was known to exist in it (Letter to Clerselier, AT IX, 205; HR II, 133; see also AT VII, 357; HR II, 211, and AT VII, 129; HR II, 30). The proof that a body cannot think and that the essence of the soul consists in thinking alone is not given, he said, until the *Sixth Meditation* (AT VII, 175; HR II, 63).

But when we turn to the passage Descartes cites from the *Sixth Meditation*, we find that he appears to

commit the very fallacy he was at pains to avoid in the
second. He says:

> Because I know that all things which I apprehend
> clearly and distinctly can be created by God as I
> apprehend them, it suffices that I am able to appre-
> hend one thing apart from another clearly and dis-
> tinctly in order to be certain that the one is different
> from the other . . . therefore, just because I know
> most certainly that I exist, and meanwhile I observe
> no other thing necessarily to pertain to my nature or
> essence, excepting that I am a thinking thing, I
> rightly conclude that my essence consists solely in
> the fact that I am a thinking thing. (AT VII, 78;
> HR I, 190)

In the *Sixth Meditation* Descartes regards himself
as entitled to draw conclusions about the real world
from the nature of his clear and distinct ideas, whereas
in the *Second Meditation* he had not yet proved that
there existed a veracious God to guarantee those ideas.
But even with this assistance, the premise established
in the *Second Meditation* will not lead to the conclusion of the Sixth. The fact that I am able to have a clear
and distinct idea of A without having a clear and distinct idea of B does not mean that I can have a clear
and distinct idea that A can exist without B. "I do not
observe that anything pertains to my essence but thinking" is not synonymous with "I observe that nothing
pertains to my essence but thinking." Descartes' sentence "I observe no other thing to pertain to my essence
except thinking" is ambiguous between these two.

Descartes continues:

Because on the one hand I have a clear and distinct idea of myself inasmuch as I am only a thinking and unextended thing, and as, on the other, I possess a distinct idea of body, inasmuch as it is only an extended and unthinking thing, it is certain that this I is entirely and absolutely distinct from my body, and can exist without it. (AT VII, 78; HR I, 190)

Here too, the argument seems to depend on the ambiguity in the phrase "clear and distinct idea of myself inasmuch as I am only a thinking and unextended thing." Does this phrase imply that I clearly and distinctly conceive that I am a thinking thing that is not extended or merely that I clearly and distinctly conceive that I am a thinking thing without conceiving that I am an extended thing? The former seems to be needed in order to establish the conclusion of the *Sixth Meditation*; the latter is the only premise that seems to be supplied by the *Second Meditation*.

Malcolm has argued that it is already established in the *Second Meditation* that I clearly and distinctly perceive that my essence is thinking and that all that is needed to complete the proof of the *Sixth Meditation* is the principle that whatever I clearly and distinctly perceive is true. In the *Second Meditation*, he claims, Descartes tacitly appeals to the following principle: "*x* is my essence if it is the case that if I am aware of *x*, then (necessarily) I am aware of myself, and if I am aware of myself, then (necessarily) I am aware of *x*." This principle, he maintains, together with the arguments explicitly formulated by Descartes, will give the conclusion that his essence is thinking.[9]

Malcolm treats "I am aware of myself" in this context as equivalent to "I am aware that I exist" and explicitly exploits the analogy between intellectual awareness and sense perception. This seems to be a dangerous procedure. Descartes is insistent that his own substance is not something he is aware of but is something known as the conclusion of an inference. "We do not have immediate awareness of substances," he wrote in the *Fourth Replies*, "rather, from the mere fact that we perceive certain forms or attributes which must inhere in something in order to have existence, we name the thing in which they exist a substance" (AT VII, 222; HR II, 98).

If, then, Malcolm is right that the *Sixth Meditation* adds nothing but the validation of clear and distinct ideas, then the *Second Meditation* must show that I clearly and distinctly perceive that the substance in which thought inheres is distinct from the substance in which extension inheres. But this it does not do. What it shows instead is that I can clearly and distinctly perceive that there exists a substance in which thought inheres without clearly and distinctly perceiving that there exists any substance in which extension inheres.

Descartes does not, in the *Second Meditation*, draw any conclusions about his essence in explicit terms; he does not state that his essence includes *at least* thinking, still less—the conclusion of the *Sixth Meditation*—that it includes *at most* thinking. But if he is ever to prove that thinking is his essence, it seems that he must prove that thinking is an inseparable property of his. If a property is any part of an essence, then it is an inseparable property. On the other hand, if he can prove that thinking is the *only* inseparable property he has, then he has proved that thinking is his essence. This will be a sufficient, but not necessary condition for thinking's being his essence; elsewhere Decartes talks as if there are inseparable properties that are not part of an essence, giving as examples existence and duration (AT VIII, 28; HR I, 242).

Although Descartes does not say in the *Second Meditation* that thinking is his essence, he does say that it is his only inseparable property. "What of thinking? I find here that thought is an attribute that belongs to me: it alone cannot be separated from me" (AT VII, 26; HR I, 151). But as we saw above when discussing this passage, "separable" in context means "deniable by a Cartesian doubter." But what is to prevent a property being inseparable from me without being indubitably inseparable from me? Certainly, if something is inseparable from me even by divine power, then it must be a necessary truth that it belongs to me; and we know that Descartes thought that even a Cartesian doubter could not doubt necessary truths. But because no necessary truth can be doubted, it does not follow that all necessary truths are known; there may be necessary truths that have never been thought of and therefore are neither doubted nor known. If Descartes' clear and distinct ideas of soul and body are to prove the separability of soul and body, then each of them must not only contain the truth about its object and not only contain nothing but the truth about its object, it must also contain the whole truth about its object. That is, they must be not only clear and distinct, but also exhaustive.

The criticisms I have put forward were first made

by Arnauld in the *Fourth Objections*. Discussing the principle that it is sufficient to be able to comprehend one thing clearly and distinctly apart from another in order to be sure that the one is diverse from the other, he wrote: ". . . in order to be true, that principle must be held to refer to the adequate notion of a thing (i.e. one which comprises everything which may be known of the thing) and not to any notion, even a clear and distinct one" (AT VII, 200; HR II, 82). And he gave a counterexample to Descartes' pattern of argument. Suppose that a man dubious about Pythagoras' theorem is looking at a right-angled triangle. Might he not argue thus? "I clearly and distinctly understand that this triangle is right-angled, without comprehending that the square on its hypotenuse is equal to the squares on its sides. Hence God at least can create a right-angled triangle, the square on the hypotenuse of which is unequal to the squares on the sides" (AT VII, 202; HR II, 83).

Descartes replied by distinguishing between adequate knowledge and complete knowledge. Knowledge known to be adequate is both unnecessary and impossible for a human being. What is necessary is not adequate knowledge but *complete* knowledge. To know something in a complete manner, we are told, is to know that it is a complete thing, and "by a complete thing I mean merely a substance endowed with those forms or attributes which suffice to let me recognize that it is a substance" (AT VII, 221; HR II, 98).

In answer to Arnauld's counterexample, Descartes maintained that his proof differed in three ways.

First, he said that the property of having the square on the hypotenuse equal to the squares on the sides is not a substance as body is—to which it may be replied that being extended is a property, and Arnauld's argument shows that being able to conceive mind without this property does not show that mind in fact lacks it.

Second, he said that though we can conceive a triangle without noting the ratio of the squares on its sides, we cannot conceive a triangle in which the squares on the sides are equal to the square on the hypotenuse without perceiving that it is right-angled. This seems simply false.

Third, he said that we cannot distinctly apprehend a triangle without knowing that there must be *some* ratio between the squares on its sides. "Now on the other hand there is nothing included in the concept of body that belongs to the mind; and nothing in that of mind that belongs to the body." The relevance of the remark about the triangle is not clear; but the remark about body and mind seems false on Descartes' own account, since the notions of substance, existence, and duration belong to mind and body alike.

Descartes seems to have had the worst of this exchange, but his cryptic remarks about *completeness* are supplemented by a letter to Gibieuf of 1642 (AT III, 472). There he explains how an idea may be an incomplete idea when it is abstracted from some more ample idea. Abstraction consists in the turning of attention from one part of an idea the better to concentrate on another. Thus, the idea of shape may be abstracted from that of extended substance; but the idea of shape is not complete, because it is impossible to think of a shape while denying that it is the shape of any extended substance. The idea of an extended substance with a shape, on the other hand, is complete since it can be conceived alone and the content of all other ideas may be denied of it.

> Now it is, it seems to me, very clear that the idea I have of a thinking thing is complete in this fashion, and that I have no other idea antecedent to it in my mind which is so joined to it that I cannot conceive them both while denying the one of the other; for if there was any such idea in me I must necessarily know it.

Thus, a distinction is drawn between adequate and complete ideas. An idea of X is adequate if it contains the whole truth about X; an idea of X is complete only if, for every Y of which I have an idea, I can clearly and distinctly conceive something that is X and not Y. The distinction is made only at the cost of making it seem unlikely that we can ever know that we have any complete ideas. To do so we would not only have to know about every idea we have, but would also have to know the relationship of every idea to every other. Elsewhere, Descartes is prepared to deny that we know every idea we have (AT III, 430), and he admits that we may discover unsuspected relationships between ideas (AT VII, 224; HR II, 100). May there not be some necessary relationship, unsuspected by Descartes, that will link his idea of thinking substance to that of extended body?

FIVE

IDEAS

I

Once Descartes has established his own existence as a conscious being, he goes on to consider the existence of God and of the external world. He proves the existence of everything except himself by examining the properties of ideas that he finds within himself. Before considering his proofs, therefore, it is worth examining what he meant by "idea."

The word "idea" is now at home in ordinary language, but it is a word, like "quality" and "intention," that was once primarily a philosophical technicality. Its modern use derives, through Locke, from Descartes; and Descartes was consciously giving it a new sense. Before him, philosophers used it to refer to archetypes in the divine intellect; it was a new departure to use it systematically for the contents of a human mind.

Descartes several times explained the sense he meant to give the word, but it is not easy to make all his explanations cohere.

One of the clearest points he made about ideas is this: "I cannot express anything in words, provided that I understand what I say, without its thereby being certain that there is within me the idea of what is signified by the words in question" (AT VII, 160; HR II, 52). This sentence may suggest that there is an idea corresponding to every significant word and that it is a sufficient condition for a man's having an idea of X that he should know how to use a word for X intelligently. Other passages give a similar impression. When an objector complained that he could not understand what was meant in the *Meditations* by the ideas of God and the soul, Descartes wrote to Mersenne that if the objector conceived anything at all when he used the words "God" and "soul" then he knew what the ideas of these things were (AT III, 393).

It seems, however, that there is no simple one-to-one correspondence between words and ideas. We are told that, strictly speaking, no idea corresponds to the word "nothing" (Interview with Burman, AT V, 153), and we learn that two ideas correspond to the word "sun" (AT VII, 39; HR I, 161). All ideas, it seems, purport to be of things: *Nullae ideae nisi tanquam rerum esse possunt* (AT VII, 44; HR I, 164). Certainly there are ideas of things of many different kinds: we hear of the ideas of God, angels, animals, and men; of sun, wax, heat, and cold; of colors, sounds, and shapes; of length, motion, and time; of thought and existence. But the idea of existence is displayed not only when I use the word "existence" but also when I say, "I exist." Some ideas seem to correspond not to particular words, but to whole sentences. Thus, Descartes speaks of ideas of "common notions"; and he gives as an example of a common notion "That which can effect what is greater or more difficult, can also accomplish what is less" (AT VII, 166; HR II, 56). But when we speak of such ideas, Descartes told Burman, we are using "idea" in a broad sense (AT V, 153). When Mersenne asked whether ideas were expressed by simple terms, Descartes replied, "I do not understand the question you ask; because words being human inventions, we can use one or more of them to express the same thing" (AT III, 417).

The circumstances that Descartes is prepared to describe as constituting the presence of an idea vary considerably from case to case. Thus, when he says that a man has an idea of God, he may mean no more than that the man has the ability to come to know God (e.g., AT IV, 187). When he speaks of having an idea of truth, he may mean understanding what truth is (e.g., AT VII, 438; HR I, 160). When he speaks of having an idea of a Syren, he may be referring to imaginative creation (*ibid.*). And when he speaks of having an idea of heat, he may be thinking of a case where someone is actually feeling the heat of a particular fire (*ibid.*). When Descartes announces the presence of an idea, therefore, he may be intending to signal anything from a remote capacity to a particular actual experience. Sometimes he speaks of ideas in general in terms appropriate to the description of capacities, as when he connects them with the ability to use words. At other times he speaks of them in terms appropriate to episodes, as when he says that ideas are "operations of the intellect" (AT VII, 232; HR II, 105).

Even when the context makes clear that what is in question is an episode and not a capacity, Descartes seems inconsistent in the manner in which he speaks of ideas. Sometimes, as in the passage just cited, an idea is an operation or act of the mind; at other times it is not so much an act of the mind as the object or *content* of such an act. This ambiguity was signaled by Descartes himself in the Preface to the *Meditations*. "In this term *idea* there is an equivocation: it may either be taken materially, as an act of my understanding . . . or objectively, as what is represented by this act" (AT VII, 8; HR I, 138).[1]

But the distinction between act and object does not solve all the difficulties latent in Descartes' terminology. There are many different relationships between acts and their objects. Some acts are identical with their objects: when I score a goal, the goal is nothing more or less than my scoring it. Some objects are produced by acts, as a poem is produced by my act when I write it. Some objects are modified by acts, as a chair is altered in color when I paint it. Other objects are objects of intentional acts, in which case the object modifies the agent instead of the agent modifying the object: when I notice a spider, that is a change in me, not in the spider.

A man's relation to his ideas is described by Descartes in verbs appropriate to acts of all these different kinds. Thus I "form" ideas (AT VII, 57; HR I, 174) or "construct" them (AT VII, 75; HR I, 188); I also "grasp" them (AT VII, 57; HR I, 175), "find" them in myself (AT VII, 63), "bring them out of" my consciousness, "as if out of a treasury" (AT VII, 64; HR I, 180); they "present themselves" to me (AT VII, 54, 75; HR I, 172) and I "notice" them (AT VII, 54, 75), "perceive" them (AT VII, 56), and my mind "looks at them" (AT VII, 73). It is difficult to decide, in any particular case, whether these locutions are just natural metaphors for such events as coming to understand a word or calling to mind a familiar face, or whether, on the other hand, they embody a particular explanatory theory of such events. When two formulations clash, have we to deal with alternative metaphors or an inconsistent theory?

The difficulties are illustrated, and in part elucidated, by two passages in letters. Both passages discuss the question of whether every man has an idea of God.

I do not doubt that all have within themselves at least an implicit idea of God, that is to say, an aptitude to perceive it explicitly; but I am not surprised that they do not feel themselves to have it, or do not notice that they have it, and perhaps will not notice it even after the thousandth reading of my meditations. (Letter to Hyperaspistes, AT III, 430)

The idea of God is so imprinted on the human mind that there is no one who does not have in himself the faculty of knowing him; but this does not prevent many people from being able to pass their whole lives without ever distinctly representing this idea to themselves. (AT IV, 187)

In both passages an idea can be a capacity (an "aptitude" or "faculty"); such an idea is called, in the first passage, an "implicit idea." But the idea of God is also something that can be "perceived" or "represented to oneself," which makes it sound like something that is the object, or the product, of a particular mental action. It is not clear, however, whether the mental action in question is coming to know what the word "God" really means or thinking a thought about God.

The ambiguities must be borne in mind in considering Descartes' famous doctrine of innate ideas. In the *Meditations* he says, "Of my ideas, some seem to be innate, some acquired, and some devised by myself" (AT VII, 38; HR I, 160). This passage suggests a classification of ideas into three kinds according to an apparent difference of origin. But when he gives examples, it seems that the ideas of the different classes are entities of different kinds quite apart from any difference in their origins. The innate ideas listed are capacities: namely, the concepts of *thing, truth,* and *thought.* The acquired ideas are particular sensations: hearing a noise, seeing the sun, feeling the fire. When Descartes says that the idea of truth is innate, he does not mean that one is born thinking of the truth; on the other hand, in saying that the idea of heat comes from the fire, he does not mean that the *concept* of heat is acquired by sensation.

The classification in the *Third Meditation* is, in any case, provisional and is elsewhere improved upon. To Mersenne Descartes wrote in 1641:

> Some ideas are adventitious, such as the idea we commonly have of the sun; others are factitious, in which class we can put the idea which the astronomers construct of the sun by their reasoning; and others are innate, such as the idea of God, Mind, Body,

triangle, and in general all those which represent true, immutable and eternal essences. (AT III, 303)

Later in the same year he wrote that an infant in its mother's womb "has in itself the ideas of God, itself, and all truths which are said to be self-evident; it has these ideas no less than adults have when they are not paying attention to them, and it does not acquire them afterwards when it grows up" (AT III, 424).

From this last statement it appears that though an unborn baby does not actually think of God, it understands very well what God is; and when it is later taught the word "God," it merely learns to give expression to a concept it has always possessed. This, however, seems to be contradicted by what Descartes wrote in 1647 in his *Notes against a Programme*: "I have never written, nor been of opinion, that the mind needs innate ideas in the sense of something different from its faculty of thinking." Ideas were innate, he explained, only

. . . in the sense of the word that we say generosity is innate in certain families; or again that in others certain diseases, e.g. gout and the stone, are innate; not that infants of these families suffer from these diseases in their mother's womb, but because they are born with a certain disposition or liability to contract them. (AT VIII, 357; HR I, 442)

But if an unborn baby has the idea of God in the same way as an adult who just happens not to be thinking of God, then the baby has something more than a mere "faculty of thinking." And what corresponds, in the case of ideas, to the "disposition or liability" to contract gout? Is it the ability to *learn* what God is? If so, then an innate idea is nothing distinct from the thinking faculty, but it is not comparable to the concept of God held by a man who has already learned what the word "God" means. Or is it the ability to *exercise* the knowledge of what God is? If so, then the unborn baby is in the same position as the instructed adult; but it cannot be said that his innate idea is nothing more than his faculty of thinking.

In a well-known passage of the *De Anima* Aristotle observed that "when a man possesses knowledge as an unexercised disposition, he is still in a state of potentiality, though not in the same way as before he learnt what he knows." [2] For instance, a man may (1) not know French at all, (2) know French but not be using his knowledge, or (3) be actually speaking French. In the first and second cases he is in "a state of potentiality" in two different ways.

Descartes, with his disdain for the Aristotelian notion of potentiality, was unable to distinguish between the unrealized capacity to acquire knowledge and the nonexercise of knowledge already acquired. There seems no real room in his system for the concept of *learning*.

Even adventitious ideas are in a sense innate, Descartes explained in the *Notes against a Programme*.

> In our ideas there is nothing which was not innate in the mind, or faculty of thinking, except only those circumstances which concern experience— the fact, for instance, that we judge this or that idea, which we now have present to our thought, is to be referred to certain extraneous things, not that these extraneous things transmitted the ideas themselves to our minds

through the organs of sense, but because they transmitted something which gave the mind occasion to
form these ideas, by means of an innate faculty, at
this time rather than at another. For nothing reaches
our mind from external objects through the organs of
sense beyond certain corporeal movements . . . but
even these movements, and the figures which arise
from them, are not conceived by us in the shape they
assume in the organs of sense . . . Hence it follows
that the ideas of the movements and figures are themselves innate in us. So much the more must the ideas
of pain, colour, sound and the like be innate, that
the mind may, on occasion of certain corporeal movements, present those ideas to itself, for they have no
likeness to the corporeal movements. (AT VIII, 358;
HR I, 443)

And to Mersenne he wrote:

I hold that all those ideas which involve no affirmation or negation are innate: for the organs of our
senses do not bring us anything which is like the
ideas which arise in us on the occasions they provide, and so that idea must have been in us before-
hand. (AT III, 417)

These passages make clear in what sense it is true
for Descartes that all ideas are innate. No matter what
X may be, the idea of X is innate in the sense that the
capacity to think of X, imagine X, feel X, experience X
is inborn in us and is not given us by the stimulus that
on a particular occasion makes us think of or experience
X. But if the idea of X is in my mind—if the innate
capacity to think of or experience X is exercised—in
such a way that I accompany the idea with a judgment

("affirmation or negation") that its occurrence is due to extramental reality, then this occurrence of the idea, this exercise of the capacity, is an *adventitious* idea. So the distinction between innate and adventitious ideas is not that there are some ideas (such as that of God) that are innate and others (such as those of heat) that are adventitious, but that one and the same idea (e.g., that of heat) is, qua capacity, innate and is, qua episode, accompanied with extramental judgment, adventitious. The judgment about the extramental reality may be that the occurrence of the idea is due to something in the world *like* the idea, in which case the adventitious idea will be confused; or it may be that the idea is caused by something of a different kind in the world, in which case the adventitious idea will be distinct (AT VIII, 33; HR I, 248).

Descartes' argument for the innateness of all ideas is based on the premise that no idea is *like* the sensory stimulus that brings it to mind. He seems to envisage only two possibilities: that ideas are innate or that they are likenesses copied from elements of the external world. "Some of my thoughts," he said in the *Third Meditation*, "are as it were pictures of objects, and these alone are properly called ideas." The comparison between ideas and pictures seems likely to mislead in the context of a discussion of innate ideas. Ideas qua capacities may plausibly be held to be innate; but capacities are not like pictures. Ideas qua objects of episodic acts may plausibly be compared to pictures before the mind; but ideas qua episodes are not innate. How far was Descartes misled by the comparison between ideas and pictures?

On the same page as he asserted that ideas were
likenesses of things, Descartes condemned as a disastrous error the belief that ideas in the mind are similar
to things outside (AT VII, 37; HR I, 160). Moreover,
in controversy with Hobbes and Gassendi he insisted
that by an idea he did not mean an image. Hobbes, for
instance, denied that we had any real idea of an angel.
"When I think of an angel, what comes into my mind
is the image sometimes of a flame, sometimes of a fair
winged child; and I feel certain that this has no likeness
to an angel, and is thus not the idea of an angel" (AT
VII, 179; HR II, 67). Descartes replied, "Here he will
have the term *idea* to mean only the images of material
things, pictured in the corporeal fancy" (AT VII, 179–
181; HR II, 67). Hobbes went on: "We have no idea at
all of the soul. We infer by reasoning that there is
something within the human body that gives it animal
motion and by means of which it feels and moves; we
call this, whatever it is, the *soul*, without having an idea
of it" (AT VII, 183; HR II, 69). Descartes retorted:
"This comes to the same as saying that there is no image
of the soul formed in our fancy, but that there is what
I call an idea" (AT VII, 183; HR II, 70). He wrote
later in similar terms to Gassendi (AT VII, 366; HR
II, 217).

This, however, does not settle the matter. In denying that ideas are images, Descartes uses "image" very
literally; he is denying not so much that ideas are mental
images as that they are cerebral images. In the definition
in the *Second Objections* he wrote: "It is not only
images pictured in the fancy that I call ideas; nay, to
such images I here decidedly refuse the title of ideas, in

so far as they are pictures in the corporeal fancy, i.e., in some part of the brain. They are ideas only in so far as they inhere in the mind itself when it is directed towards that part of the brain" (AT VII, 161; HR II, 52).[3]

Descartes believed, then, that the exercise of the imagination or fancy—I use the latter term to correspond to his technical term *"phantasia"*—consisted in looking at pictures in the brain. In consequence, when he denies that ideas are images, we cannot be quite sure that he is denying that ideas are mental images in the sense of pictures in the mind's eye. For mental images are not material pictures in the brain. Mental images are indeed in one sense material. There can be mental pictures only of things of which there can be real pictures: primarily, of material objects and things perceptible by sight. There can, of course, be mental pictures of justice or eternity, just as there can be painted pictures of these things, but any mental picture of an abstract entity must represent it by representing first of all something perceptible, like a pair of scales or a white circle. Again, mental images, like material pictures, last for periods of time and have spatial parts such as a top and a bottom and a left-hand and right-hand side. But mental images are immaterial in another sense. They are not made out of any stuff, however tenuous. Unlike material pictures, they do not exist unless before the mind, nor can they have properties that pass unperceived. Having mental images is no doubt connected with events in the brain; but to have an image is not to *perceive* any cerebral entity. What Descartes said of his ideas is true also of mental images, that they are not "composed of any matter" (AT VII, 232; HR II, 105).

It is customary nowadays to distinguish between mental images and concepts. To have a concept of X is to know what X is: knowledge that is expressed, for instance, in the ability to distinguish between what is X and what is not X, or in the ability to use a word for X in some language. One and the same concept, in this sense, may be exercised when different images are in the mind, and the same image may be the vehicle for several concepts. When Descartes insists against his critics on the distinction between images and ideas, it looks *prima facie* as if he is marking off mental images from concepts. In part, no doubt, he is; that is, some of the criteria by which he is drawing his distinction are the same as the criteria by which we make our distinction. But, in fact, his ideas have some of the properties of material pictures, some of the properties of mental images, and some of the properties of concepts. Like material and mental pictures, they are representations that exhibit things. Like mental pictures, and unlike cerebral pictures, they are not made out of any matter. Unlike either, they can represent immaterial things (e.g., God) without doing so by representing something material (e.g., a bearded sage). Like material pictures, but unlike mental images, they exist even when not before the mind, and when before the mind they can contain details that the mind has not noticed.

In all these respects Descartes' ideas are unlike concepts. The acquisition and use of a concept cannot be described as if it were like the acquisition or inspection of a representation. The ability to recognize a man, which is part of the possession of the concept of *man*, cannot be explained by postulating the presence of a representation of a man against which any alleged man can be checked for correspondence, for the representation would itself have to be correctly recognized each time it presented itself to consciousness. If a further representation is needed to explain this ability, we are started on a vicious regress; if not, then no representation need have been postulated in the first place.

If we are to evaluate Descartes' claim that the intelligent use of words presupposes the presence of innate ideas, we must make several distinctions. That the intelligent use of words presupposes the possession of concepts is correct; that it presupposes the presence of something like a picture is incorrect. The quasi-pictures Descartes postulates are neither necessary nor sufficient to explain the intelligent use of words; moreover, they are intrinsically incoherent entities, combining as they do the properties of material and immaterial images. That the concepts exercised in the intelligent use of words are not acquired on the occasions of their use is correct; that they are inborn is incorrect. In general, the concepts expressed in words are acquired when language is learned; what is inborn is not the concepts themselves but the ability to acquire them, the faculty of linguistic intelligence in which men surpass other animals.

In any argument in which Descartes employs the term "idea" we have to ask ourselves whether he means an act or its object, and whether he means a mental image, the exercise of a concept, or the occurrence of an experience. Having done so, we have to check whether the premises of his arguments are true and whether his conclusions follow if the interpretation of "idea" is held constant throughout. Such a procedure often throws light not only on Descartes' own theses about ideas but on the arguments brought against them by later critics such as the British empiricists.

II

We must turn to the relation between the notion of "idea" and some of the other technical terms of Descartes' philosophy. What is the relation, for instance, between ideas and thoughts? "*Cogitatio*" shares some of the ambiguities of "idea." To Hobbes, Descartes wrote: "Thought is taken sometimes for an act, sometimes for a faculty, and sometimes for the subject possessing the faculty" (AT VII, 174; HR II, 62). When he discusses the relationships between ideas and thoughts, however, commonly he seems to be taking both words in their episodic senses as conscious events.

Occasionally the words "idea" and "thought" are used as synonyms (e.g., AT VI, 559; HR I, 102; Letter to Clerselier, AT V, 354); elsewhere, ideas are described as "*modi cogitandi,*" modes of thought or ways of thinking (e.g., AT VII, 40, 44; HR I, 161). In Descartes' fullest definition of "idea," an idea is said to be the form of a thought: "By the word 'idea' I mean the form of any thought, that form by the immediate awareness of which I am conscious of that said thought" (AT VII, 160; HR II, 52). The word "form" is a piece of scholastic jargon, but no scholastic theory seems to be involved. By calling ideas "forms" Descartes seems to mean simply that they are nonmaterial representations of things (AT VII, 232; HR II, 105). In the *Third Meditation*, when Descartes has said that only those of his thoughts that are like pictures really deserve the name of "idea," he goes on to say:

> Other thoughts have other forms in addition (*aliae vero alias quasdam praeterea formas habent*): when I will, am afraid, assert or deny, there is always something which I take as the topic of my thought; but my thought comprises more than the likeness of the thing in question; of these experiences, some are termed volitions or emotions, others are termed judgements. (AT VII, 37; HR I, 159)

This passage gives the impression that the pure thought of X, the desire for X, and the fear of X all involve the idea of X; but the first consists of this idea alone, while the second and third consist of the same idea plus something extra.

Is this something extra itself an idea? The natural way of reading the passage suggests that it is not. What makes the difference between the thought of X and the fear of X is not itself an idea, though it is like an idea in being a "form." However, this would make it difficult to understand the definition of "idea" quoted above from the *Second Objections*. For there it is said that it is by the awareness of the idea that I am conscious of a thought; but awareness merely of the idea of X will not suffice to make me conscious that I fear X.

This difficulty puzzled Hobbes, who wrote:

> When anybody wills or is afraid, he has an image of the thing he fears or the action he wills; what more is comprised in the thought of one who wills or is

afraid is not explained. Fear is a thought, but so far
as I can see it can only be the thought of the thing
a man fears. What is fear of an onrushing lion but
the idea of an onrushing lion together with the effect
that this idea produces in the heart, which leads the
one who fears to make the animal motion called
running away? Now the motion of running away is
not a thought. (AT VII, 182; HR II, 68)

Descartes replied brusquely:

It is obvious that seeing a lion and at the same time
fearing it is different from just seeing . . .

but in an earlier reply to Hobbes he had given a more
instructive answer.

I take the term "idea" to stand for whatever the
mind is directly aware of (a *mente perciptitur*). For
instance, when I will or am afraid, I am at the same
time aware of (*percipio*) willing or being afraid;
thus I count *volition* and *fear* among ideas. (AT VII,
181; HR II, 68)

This answer is still not decisive. Does he mean by
the last sentence that there are, among ideas, ideas *of*
volition and ideas *of* fear, so that when I fear a lion
there are simultaneously present in my mind the idea of
a lion and the idea of fear? Or does he mean that volition and fear are themselves ideas, so that the fear of a
lion is just a special kind of idea of a lion—as it were,
a picture of a lion in a particular color appropriate to
fear? The former account seems to fit better the description of fear in the *Passions of the Soul* (AT XI,
359; HR I, 350), though there the terminology of ideas
is not used. But the latter seems to square better with

some remarks on volition in a letter of 1641. "I claim that we have ideas not only of everything which is in our intellect, but also of everything which is in the will. For we cannot will anything without knowing that we will it, nor know it, except by an idea; but I do not claim that this idea is different from the action itself" (AT III, 295).

Perhaps it is possible to reconcile these contrasting statements in the following way. Whenever I am conscious of X or think of X, then I have an idea of X. If X is something other than my own mental activity—say, the heat of the fire, or God—then this idea is something distinct from X that represents X. If X is one of my own mental activities—say, willing or fearing—then I am directly aware of X; that is to say, the idea of X is not a representation of X, but is X itself. If I think of a lion, my thought simply is the occurrence of the idea of a lion in my mind, and I am aware of my thinking simply by perceiving that idea. (Thinking being a mental activity, I need no further representation—no idea of the idea of a lion—to perceive the thinking.) On the other hand, if I am afraid of a lion, there occurs in my mind not only the idea of the lion, but also the fear. There is, in one sense, no idea of the fear; that is, there is no representation of the fear, distinct from the fear itself, present in the mind. But as the fear is itself directly perceptible, on Descartes' theory, and because an idea is that by which something is made conscious, the fear itself can be called an idea. Thus, that which differentiates being afraid of the lion from merely thinking of the lion, in one sense is, and in another sense is not, an idea. Here we meet again the ambiguity of "idea" as between act and object; it is the idea of a lion qua act of the mind, and not qua object of such an act, that can be said to be identical with my thinking of a lion.

It is time to investigate further the notion of "object." So far, we have been considering ideas as properties or events in the mind that has them. It is also possible to look at them from a reverse point of view. When I see the sun, the sun is seen by me. If I begin to think of the sun, then at the same time the sun begins to have a new property, namely, the property of being thought of by me. The sun, we might quite naturally say, comes into my mind. This, we may feel, is not a very important property of the sun, nor one very intimately connected with it; but still, it is a genuine property of the real sun: a relationship between it and my mind. Scholastics contemporary with Descartes spoke of this property as that of "being 'objectively' in the understanding"—"objectively" meaning "as an object of thought." Thus, they would say that when I have an idea of the sun, the sun is "objectively" in my understanding.

Descartes adopted this mode of speaking so far as it concerned clear and distinct ideas (AT VII, 233; HR II, 106). A marginal note to the Latin *Discourse of Method* reads: "The noun 'Idea' is generally used for everything which is thought of (*res cogitata*), insofar as it has only a certain objective existence in the intellect" (AT VI, 559). But for Descartes, the *res cogitata* that exists in my mind when I think of the sun is not the sun itself, but some proxy for the sun. The scholastic Caterus, objecting to Descartes' manner of investigating the causes of ideas, wrote:

What is an idea? It is the thing thought of itself in
so far as that is "objectively in the understanding."
But what is "existing objectively in the understanding"? As I was taught, it is simply being the object
of an act of thought, which is merely an external
attribute of the thing and adds no reality to it. (AT
VII, 92; HR II, 2)

The sun's being seen, or coming into my mind, is no
real change in the sun.

Descartes' reply is very illuminating.

He refers to the thing itself, which is as it were
placed outside the understanding, and respecting
which it is certainly an extrinsic attribute to be
objectively in the understanding; but what I speak
of is the idea, which never exists outside the mind,
and in the case of which "objective existence" means
precisely being in the understanding in the way in
which objects are normally there. Thus, for example,
if someone asks what happens to the sun when it
exists objectively in my understanding, it is correct
to reply that it acquires nothing but a merely extrinsic attribute, that of providing the object with
which my thought is concerned. But if the question
be, what the idea of the sun is, and the answer be
given that it is the thing thought of (*res cogitata*)
in so far as it exists objectively in the understanding,
then no one will think that it is the sun itself with
its merely external attribute. And in this case "objective existence in the understanding" will not mean
merely providing the object with which my thought
is concerned, but existing in the understanding in
the way in which its objects normally exist there.
Hence the idea of the sun will be the sun itself
existing in the understanding, not indeed formally,

as it exists in the sky, but objectively, i.e. in the way in which objects normally exist in the mind. (AT VII, 102; HR II, 9)

In this passage we can see clearly a certain reduplication taking place. "To think of the sun" may be rephrased, if you like, as "to have an idea of the sun." But to think of the sun is not the same as to think of an idea of the sun; and so "to think of an idea of the sun" is not the same as "to have an idea of the sun." If I think of the sun, then the sun is thought of by me; and "the sun is thought of by me" can be rephrased, if you like, as "the sun has an objective existence in me." Putting our two rephrasings together, we can say that whenever I have an idea of the sun, the sun has objective existence in me; we can even say that my having an idea of the sun and the sun's having objective existence in me are one and the same thing. But that is not the same as saying, as Descartes does, that when I have an idea of the sun, an idea of the sun has objective existence in me. For if we decode this, it means that when I think of the sun, I think of an idea of the sun. This has not been proved and is indeed false. An extra entity has been spirited into existence; and this comes out in the way Descartes actually contradicts himself, saying first that what exists in the mind in the way in which objects exist in the mind is not the sun, but the idea of the sun, and then going on to say that the idea of the sun is the sun itself existing in the mind in the way in which objects normally exist in the mind.

III

Ideas, according to Descartes, may have various properties. Of these, two types are most important. First, an idea may be true or false, and second, it may be either clear and distinct or obscure and confused.

Descartes quite often speaks of ideas as being true or false, but in the *Third Meditation* he says:

> Ideas considered in themselves, and not referred to something else, cannot strictly speaking be false; whether I imagine a she-goat or a chimera, it is not less true that I imagine one than the other. Again, falsehood is not to be feared in the will or the emotions; I may desire what is evil, or what does not exist anywhere, but it is none the less true that I desire it. Only judgements remain: it is here that I must take precaution against falsehood. (AT VII, 37; HR I, 159)

This seems an odd piece of reasoning. Could one not as well argue that judgments in themselves could not be false, on the grounds that whether I judge the sun to be larger than the earth or judge it to be smaller than the earth, it is nonetheless true that I judge? A false judgment is a real judgment, so you cannot prove that the imagination of a chimera is not a false imagination by showing that it is a real imagination. However, it is true that the imagination of a chimera is not made a false imagination by the fact that there is no such thing as a chimera, and that the wish for a chimera is not made a false wish by the same fact; whereas the chimera's nonexistence does make false a judgment that here is a chimera. Moreover, the idea of a chimera is no less the idea *of a chimera* than the idea of a goat is the idea of a goat. Again, the desire for Utopia is a desire for nothing less than Utopia itself, even though there is no such place as Utopia. Perhaps this is the point Descartes wished to make. But would he have said that a judgment about God, if there is no God, is not really a judgment about God?

However this may be, with regard to truth and falsity, ideas can be defective in two ways. First, an idea may not be a real idea (*vera idea, idée veritable*). We have no real idea of immobility, or darkness, or nothingness; we conceive these things by negation only (AT VII, 45; HR I, 166). Second, an idea can be materially false: it can, he says, "represent what is not a thing as if it were a thing." Suppose, for instance, that cold is merely the absence of heat, and I take it for a reality in its own right. In that case I have a "materially false" idea of cold. Descartes explained to Burman:

> There can be matter for error, even if I do not refer my ideas to anything outside me, since I can be mistaken about their nature. For instance, if I considered the idea of colour and said that it was a thing, a quality—or rather that colour itself, which is represented by that idea, is something of the kind; for instance, if I said that whiteness is a quality, even if I did not refer this idea to anything outside me, even if I said or supposed that there was not a single white object, none the less I might make a mistake in abstract, about whiteness itself and its nature or idea. (AT V, 152)

(Color, for Descartes, was not a real quality, the sensation of color being caused by the action of subtle matter on the optic nerve; cf. below, p. 217.)

This notion of "materially false" ideas puzzled Arnauld. If cold is just an absence, he said, then there can be no positive idea of it, and hence no false idea of it. "What does that idea of cold, which you say is false materially, display to your mind? Absence? In that case, it is a true idea. A positive reality? Then it is not the idea of cold" (AT VII, 206; HR II, 87). Descartes insisted in reply that the idea of cold "furnishes me with material for error, if in fact cold is an absence and does not possess so much reality as heat, because when I consider either of the ideas of heat and cold just as I received them both from the senses, I am unable to perceive that more reality is represented to me by one than by the other" (AT VII, 232; HR II, 105). The ideas of heat and cold "are referred to something other than that of which they are in truth the ideas." Thus, if cold is the mere absence of heat, "the idea of cold is not cold itself existing objectively in the understanding, but some other thing which is wrongly taken for that absence, namely, some sensation which has no existence outside the mind" (AT VII, 233; HR II, 106).

Several things are confusing in Descartes' account of false ideas. First of all, the same word, *"vera"* is used to mark the distinction between genuine ideas and negations and the distinction between true and false ideas. The two distinctions are not the same; the idea of cold is a genuine idea, but a materially false one. All genuine ideas are, "as it were, of things" (*tanquam rerum*); true ideas really are ideas of things (*rerum quarundam ideae*); false ideas are ideas of nonthings (*non rerum*) (AT VII, 43; HR I, 164). Perhaps Descartes means the order of words to be significant: "*vera idea*" will mean "genuine idea," and "*idea vera*" will mean "true idea." (Contrast AT VII, 45, l. 24 with AT VII, 46, ll. 5 ff.)

Second, what does Descartes think that the idea of cold is really an idea *of*? He says that it is "referred to something other than that of which it is in truth the idea." "To refer an idea to something" means, in Descartes' terminology, "to judge that some extramental existent is similar to the idea." Such a judgment, in the case of cold, Descartes believed to be false; there is no extramental existent similar to the idea of cold. The correct judgment would be that the idea is a sensation that has no existence outside the mind. In that case, it seems, the idea cannot be the idea *of* anything but itself.

Throughout the exchange with Arnauld, Descartes appears to be confused about the criterion for the object of an idea. What is it that makes a particular idea the idea *of cold*? Is it the idea's resembling cold? Or is it the idea's being meant by its possessor to resemble cold?

The question recalls Descartes' comparison between ideas and pictures. It corresponds to the question "What makes a particular picture a picture *of Napoleon*?" Is it the picture's resembling Napoleon? Or is it the picture's being meant by the painter to resemble Napoleon—for example, having "Napoleon" as its caption? In this case the answer seems clear. A picture is a picture of Napoleon if it is meant to resemble Napoleon; and if it does not in fact resemble Napoleon, then it is a bad likeness. Clearly, Arnauld would be foolish to argue that there could not be a poor portrait of Napoleon, on the ground that any portrait was either like Napoleon, and therefore a good portrait, or unlike Napoleon, and therefore not a portrait of Napoleon at all.

Descartes, it seems, cannot give a consistent answer to the question about the criterion for the object of an idea. The idea of cold does not resemble cold. Nonetheless, it really is the idea of cold. The criterion that settles this, then, cannot be its resembling cold, but must be its being believed by its possessor to resemble cold, that is, its being "referred to cold." On the other hand, if an idea is the idea *of* whatever it is "referred" to, then it cannot be the case that the idea of cold is referred to something other than that of which it is in truth the idea. Once again, the comparison between ideas and pictures has led Descartes into incoherence.

The most important properties Descartes attributes to ideas are, besides truth and falsity, those of clarity (versus obscurity) and distinctness (versus confusedness). To conclude this treatment of ideas in Descartes I wish to consider the exact nature of these properties as applied to simple ideas such as sensations, without for the moment considering the epistemological use Descartes makes of the principle that whatever is clearly and distinctly perceived is true.

The fullest account of clarity and distinctness is given in the *Principles*.

> The knowledge upon which a certain and incontrovertible judgement can be formed, should not alone be clear but also distinct. I term that clear which is present and apparent to an attentive mind, in the

same way as we assert that we see objects clearly when, being present to the regarding eye, they operate upon it with sufficient strength. But the distinct is that which is so precise and different from all other objects that it contains within itself nothing but what is clear. When, for instance, a severe pain is felt, the perception of this pain may be very clear, and yet for all that not distinct, because it is usually confused by the sufferers with the obscure judgement that they form upon its nature, assuming as they do that something exists in the part affected, similar to the sensation of pain of which they are alone clearly conscious. (AT VIII, 21; HR I, 237)

We are told, however, that we may have a clear knowledge of our sensations if we take care to include in the judgments we form of them only that which we know to be precisely contained in our perception of them and of which we are intimately conscious. Thus, "there is no reason that we should be obliged to believe that the pain, for example, which we feel in our foot, is anything beyond our mind which exists in our foot." We can avoid error if we judge that there is something, of whose nature we are ignorant, that causes the sensation of pain in our minds (AT VIII, 32; HR I, 247).

There seem here to be three separate elements in Descartes' account: the pain, the perception of the pain, and the judgment about the pain. The perception of the pain seems to be something distinct from the pain, for there are properties such as clarity and distinctness that belong to the perception, but not to the pain. The perception seems to be something distinct from the judgment; judgment is an act of the will that is in our power to make or withhold, and we are enjoined to restrict our judgment to what we clearly and distinctly perceive. But it is not at all easy to work out what Descartes considers to be the relationships between these three.

Insofar as pain is a *cogitatio*, it would seem that pain cannot occur without being perceived. Can it, however, occur without being perceived clearly? Descartes seems to give two different answers to this. On the one hand, he says that "when a man feels great pain, he has a very clear perception of pain"; on the other hand, he says that we have a clear perception of our sensations only if we carefully restrict our judgment about them and that "this is a condition most difficult to observe." If we ask, however, whether a pain may be perceived distinctly, the answer is plain. "A perception may be clear without being distinct, though not distinct without being clear" (AT VIII, 22; HR I, 237). Again, Descartes seems explicit enough on the relationship between perception and judgment. Judgment differs from perception in being an act of the will, in being concerned with extramental reality, and in being liable to error. The faculty of perceiving is infallible, that of assenting can err (AT VIII, 21; HR I, 236). Judgment may occur without perception; that is precisely the cause of error: "people form judgments about what they do not perceive and thus fall into error" (AT VIII, 21; HR I, 236). What of the converse case? Can clear and distinct perception occur without judgment? Here there are some puzzles. On the one hand, we learn that "we are by nature so disposed to give our assent to things that we clearly perceive, that we cannot possibly doubt of their truth" (AT VIII, 21; HR I, 236). Yet on the other hand, does not the whole procedure of methodic doubt suppose that one can withhold one's judgment even about what seems most clear?

When we examine Descartes' doctrines closely, the reason for the inconsistencies seems to be this: The clear and distinct perception of pain is not in fact identifiable separately from the occurrence of pain and the judgment about the origin of the pain.

First, to perceive a pain clearly simply is to have a severe pain. Descartes says: "I call clear that which is present and manifest to an attentive mind; just as we are said to see clearly objects when they are present and operate strongly, and when our eyes are in the right disposition to survey them" (AT VII, 22; HR I, 237). Here there seem to be two elements in clarity: that the object of perception be manifest and that the perceiving faculty be attentive. In the case of sight, such a distinction is possible; in the case of pain, it is illusory. Descartes nowhere suggests what would be the difference between the unclear perception of a manifest pain and the clear perception of an obscure pain. Yet it must be possible to make out such a difference if the distinction between the occurrence of a pain and the perception of a pain is to be a genuine one.

Second, to perceive a pain distinctly is simply to make the correct judgment about one's pain. It is to make the correct, cautious, judgment "what I feel is caused by I know not what," rather than the incorrect, rash judgment "what I feel is something in my foot." The difference between a distinct and a confused perception is explained precisely in terms of the nature of the accompanying judgment. When the perception of pain is not distinct, that is because it is "confused by the sufferers with the obscure judgement that they form upon its nature" (AT III, 21; HR I, 237).

The perception of pain, then, is not a genuine intermediary between the occurrence of pain and the judgment on pain. Of the two properties of the perception, one, clarity, is really a property of the pain that occurs, and the other, distinctness, is really a property of the judgment made about it.

The incoherence noted in the *Principles* is to be found also in the *Third Meditation*. Sometimes, there, clarity and distinctness are properties of our perception of ideas and thoughts (AT VII, 35, 34; HR I, 158), a perception described as "looking with the eyes of the mind" (AT VII, 36, 35); sometimes they are properties of what is looked at, the idea itself (AT VII, 43, 31; HR I, 164). In particular the idea of God is itself clear and distinct (AT VII, 46, 15; HR I, 166); its elements are clearly and distinctly *perceived* (AT VII, 46, 17; HR I, 166). This reduplication is the fruit of the ambiguity of "idea," which means sometimes an act and sometimes its object. That ambiguity, as we have said, was pointed out by Descartes himself; but he did not realize that it had fatal consequences for his epistemology.

SIX

THE
IDEA
OF
GOD

In Descartes' first proof of the existence of God he establishes that he has an idea of God, that is, of a supreme, perfect, eternal, infinite, omniscient, almighty creator. He then considers the origin of this idea and, having rejected various hypotheses, comes to the conclusion that it must have been placed in him by an actually existent perfect being. The proof is stated briefly in the fourth part of the *Discourse* (AT VI, 34; HR I, 102), in great detail in the *Third Meditation* (AT VII, 40–48; HR 1, 161–167), and again more succinctly in the *Principles* (AT VIII, 11–12; HR I, 225–226). It is stated most formally, *more geometrico*, in an appendix to the *Second Replies* (AT VII, 167; HR II, 57).

Since Kant, arguments for the existence of God

have been classified as cosmological or ontological, according to whether they start from items in the world or from the concept of Godhead. Descartes is one of the principal exponents of the classical ontological argument, which he presented in the *Fifth Meditation*. The proof in the *Third Meditation*, though it starts from Descartes' idea of God, is in fact a cosmological argument, since it treats that idea as an effect that can be explained only by a divine cause. Like Aquinas, Descartes thinks it possible to prove the existence of God from a consideration of God's creatures. But whereas Aquinas starts from the visible world, Descartes must base his proof only on his own mind and its ideas. For until he is assured of God's existence and veracity, he has no guarantee that the external world exists at all.[1]

The most concise statement of the proof is as follows:

> Because we find in ourselves the idea of a God, or a supremely perfect Being, we are able to investigate the cause which produces this idea in us; but after, on considering the immensity of the perfection it possesses, we are constrained to consider it only as emanating from an all perfect being, that is from a God who truly exists. (AT VIII, 11; HR I, 226)

The first step announces the presence of the idea of God. This seems taken for granted in the *Third Meditation*, where the thought of God appears in the first list of things rightly to be called "ideas" (AT VII, 37; HR I, 159; cf. also AT VII, 43, 45). Critics, including Hobbes and Gassendi, denied that we had any real idea of God. Descartes often countered such critics with an argument *ad hominem*: if they understood what their

words meant when they talked about God, then they
had an idea of God. Everyone, he believed, had an
innate idea of God; but this idea might remain implicit,
might remain an unactualized capacity to know God
(AT III, 393; AT IV, 187). Though a man cannot fail
to know what is actually in his mind, he may not know
every capacity in his mind; hence, it is not surprising if
some people deny that they have an idea of God (Letter
to Hyperaspistes, AT III, 430).

Descartes' critics, however, were not merely appealing to their own lack of awareness of an idea of God
in themselves. They gave reasons for their denial. Hobbes argued that there could be no idea of God, because
no image could be made of God. Descartes replied that
an idea was not an image (AT VII, 180–181; HR II, 67–
68). Gassendi insisted that a finite intellect was incapable of conceiving the infinite; any human idea purporting to be an idea of God was no better than an idea
of an elephant modeled on observation of a flea (AT
VII, 287–288; HR II, 158–159). At most we can be
said to know part of the infinite, not the infinite itself.
"Would it not be a fine likeness of me if the painter
were to depict a single one of my hairs, or even the tip
of a single hair? Yet what we know of an infinite God
is in proportion infinitely less than the tip of a single
hair in comparison with myself" (AT VII, 297; HR II,
166). In reply, Descartes drew a distinction between
understanding the infinite and comprehending the infinite. We can understand God in our fashion, and so
we have an idea of Him; but we cannot comprehend
Him, so we have no adequate idea of Him. Nonetheless,
our idea is not an idea of a *part* of the infinite. A

beginner at geometry does not know all that there is to
know about a triangle; nonetheless he has an idea of a
whole triangle. "Just as it suffices to understand a figure
bounded by three lines in order to have an idea of a
whole triangle; so it is sufficient to understand a thing
bounded by no limits in order to have a true and complete idea of the whole of the infinite" (AT VII, 365–
368; HR II, 216–218).

In controversy and in exposition Descartes proved
the idea of God from discourse about God (AT VII,
160, 167; HR II, 52, 57); in private meditation he established its presence without appealing to the existence of
bodies or other minds. "When I consider that I doubt,
that is to say that I am an incomplete and dependent
being, there comes before my mind the idea of a being
which is independent and complete, that is, of God"
(AT VII, 46, 53; HR I, 166, 171). Out of the hat of the
cogito yet another rabbit is produced.

[margin handwriting: Quote 2 from paper]

We might set the argument out in steps as follows:

(1) I am in doubt about some things.
(2) I lack at least one perfection.
(3) I am not altogether perfect.
(4) I know I am not altogether perfect.
(5) I know what "not altogether perfect" means.
(6) I know what "altogether perfect" means.
(7) I have an idea of absolute perfection, that is,
    of God.

Step (2) follows from (1) in conjunction with the
premises that to doubt is to lack knowledge and that
knowledge is a perfection. Step (3) seems to follow
straightforwardly from (2), and reflection on (1), (2),

and (3) puts Descartes in a position to affirm (4). Step (5) seems an obvious corollary of (4); (6) follows from (5) in conjunction with the premise that one cannot know what a predicate "not F" means without knowing what the predicate "F" means. This seems difficult to reject: knowing what "not red" means seems to involve knowing what "red" means. Step (7) follows from (6) in conjunction with Descartes' principle that if one can use an expression meaningfully one has the appropriate idea (AT III, 393).

Despite its plausibility the argument is unsatisfactory as can be seen from the following parallel:

(8) I am not triangular.
(9) I lack at least one shape.
(10) I am not omniform (i.e., I do not have every shape).
(11) I know I am not omniform.
(12) I know what "not omniform" means.
(13) I know what "omniform" means.
(14) I have an idea of an omniform being (i.e., a being with every possible shape).

The argument fails to establish what Descartes wants because of the ambiguity of "idea." Both (7) and (14) are true, provided that to have an idea is simply to know what the words expressing the idea mean. It is possible for me to have an idea in this sense without the idea's being coherent, as (14) shows. But if so, then (7) in no way shows that I have a clear and distinct idea of God; because in order to be clear and distinct an idea must at the very least be coherent (AT VII, 117; HR II, 20). For all that this argument shows, the idea of a being possessing every perfection may be as nonsensical as the idea of a being possessing every possible shape.

However, Descartes has a number of other arguments to show that the idea of God is not an incoherent idea but a truly clear and distinct idea. All these arguments depend on a single premise: ". . . the idea by which I understand a supreme God, eternal infinite, omniscient, omnipotent, and Creator of all things outside himself, has certainly more objective reality . . . than any other idea" (AT VII, 40, 46; HR I, 162, 166). To understand this, we must grasp Descartes' theory of objective reality.

"When we reflect," he says, "on the various ideas that are in us, it is easy to perceive that there is not much difference between them when they are considered only as modes of thinking; but they are widely different in another way, since the one represents one thing, and the other another" (AT VIII, 11; HR I, 226). Insofar as they represent different things, ideas are said to differ in objective reality. "By the objective reality of an idea I mean the being of the thing represented in the idea, as it occurs in the idea. . . . whatever we perceive as being in the objects of our ideas is in the ideas themselves objectively" (AT VII, 161; HR II, 52). If my idea represents something that is F, then the idea contains objective F-ness; thus, the idea of a red hen contains objective redness. When we consider ideas as modes of thought, we are considering their *formal* or *actual* properties; their objective properties are those that belong to them in virtue of their representative nature. "Objective reality," which for Descartes signified something mental, has come by a quirk of history to be synonymous with "extramental existence." For this reason some translators render Descartes' contrast between the objective and the formal by the pair of terms "representative" and "inherent." [2] Despite the dangers, I shall use the traditional transliterations.

The distinction between the formal and the objective properties of ideas is a valid and useful one. It may be illustrated by reference to a property Descartes does not himself mention in this context, namely, temporal location. When I in 1966 think of the battle fought at Hastings in 1066, the formal time of my idea is 1966; its objective time is 1066. One of Descartes' own examples is the property of *ingeniousness*. If I think about an ingenious machine, then my idea has the property of objective ingeniousness (AT VIII, 11; HR I, 226). But of course it may lack the property of formal ingeniousness: it may be a vague and inaccurate idea of a machine whose workings I do not understand. Perhaps Descartes did not sufficiently reflect on this possibility when he discussed our idea of God.

Descartes applied his theory of objective properties to ideas involving scalar magnitudes. If one idea represents something that is more F than what is represented by another idea, then the first idea has more objective F-ness—is more objectively F—than the second. Thus, if A is more perfect than B, the idea of A is more objectively perfect than the idea of B. Analogously, it would seem, if A is larger than B, then the idea of A is objectively larger than the idea of B. Similarly, a picture of an elephant would be objectively larger than a picture of a flea. This is, of course, perfectly compatible with the elephant picture's being actually or formally smaller than the flea picture.

Among the scalar magnitudes to which Descartes applied his theory was that of *reality*. "There are diverse degrees of reality or being (*entitas*)," he explained, "for substance has more reality than accident or mode; and infinite substance has more than finite substance. Hence there is more objective reality in the idea of substance than in that of accident; more in the idea of infinite than of finite substance" (AT VII, 165; HR II, 56). Hobbes objected that reality did not admit of degrees: how can one thing be more a thing than another thing? Descartes simply repeated his earlier explanation and added that "if there be real qualities or incomplete substances, they are things to a greater extent than modes are, but less than complete substances" (AT VII, 185; HR II, 71).

We sometimes use the word "reality" to distinguish fact from fiction: on this view, the idea of a lion would have more objective reality than the idea of a unicorn, since lions exist and unicorns do not. But this is not what Descartes means. We can imagine, he says, that God does not exist; but we cannot imagine that the idea of Him represents nothing real (AT VII, 46; HR I, 166).

To be real is to be a thing, a *res*. Repeatedly Descartes rejects the scholastic theory of accidents, to which he alluded in his reply to Hobbes, on the ground that if accidents are real they are substances and so not accidents. "It is altogether inconceivable that there should be real accidents, because whatever is real, can exist independently of any other subject; and whatever can exist thus separately is a substance" (AT VII, 434; HR II, 250). Reality, therefore, means substantiality in the sense of *independence*.

So considered, reality does not admit of degrees. Descartes' scale of being is not the medieval hierarchy of God, angels, men, beasts, plants, matter. It has only three points: infinite substance, finite substance, and modes. But the way in which modes depend on substance is not the same as that in which finite substances depend on the infinite substance. Modes are logically dependent on substance; they "inhere in it as subject." Statements with modes for their subjects must be translatable into statements with substances for their subjects, as statements about the Cheshire Cat's smile must be translatable into statements about the Cheshire Cat. Created substances are not logically, but causally, dependent on God. They do not inhere in God as subject, but are effects of God as creator. Thus, there is no uniform property of independence which things might possess to a greater or less degree.

Perfection, no less than reality, is treated by Descartes as scalar. Sometimes he used the word "perfection" as a synonym for "reality," in which case his practice is open to the objection just made (e.g., AT VII, 40; HR I, 162). Sometimes he speaks of "perfections" in the plural, so that A is more perfect than B if A has more perfections than B (e.g., AT VII, 46; HR I, 166). This is tolerable only if no two perfections are incompatible with each other, which requires proof. Sometimes again A is said to be more perfect than B if A is more F than B, where "F" signifies some particular perfection (*ibid.*). This is reasonable only if what "F" signifies is itself scalar, in the way that intelligence may be thought to be.

"I must not imagine," says Descartes, "that I do not perceive the infinite by a true idea, but only by the negation of the finite." How is one to decide whether an idea or thought is positive or negative? It cannot be by seeing whether the expression of the idea contains a negative particle or not; in that case, the idea that grass is green would be a different idea from the idea that grass is no. not green. Gottlob Frege once wrote: "Consider the sentences 'Christ is immortal', 'Christ lives for ever', 'Christ is not immortal', 'Christ is mortal', 'Christ does not live for ever'. Now which of the thoughts we have here is affirmative, which negative?" [3] Similarly, when we have the sentences "God is perfect," "God is real," "God is independent," "God is infinite," we cannot settle which of the ideas expressed is positive and which negative by looking for the presence or absence of the negative prefix "in." In fact, it seems that there is no way of sorting predicates into positive and negative in the manner required by Descartes' argument. He says that we perceive rest by the negation of movement; but one could as well say that we perceive movement by the negation of rest. He says also that we perceive darkness by the negation of light. This makes his view more plausible, because it was a genuine discovery that darkness was the absence of light and not some tangible opposite that moved into any place vacated by light. But the discovery that "there is darkness here" was equivalent to "there is no light here" did not mean that the ability to detect when there is light present was in some way prior to the ability to detect when there is no light. The two abilities are one and the same.

To prove that the idea of God cannot be a negation, Descartes appeals to the argument from doubting we considered earlier. I could not know I was imperfect, he argues, if I did not already have the idea of a more perfect being; but—he tacitly assumes—the positive is always prior to the negative; therefore, the idea of God's perfection cannot be the mere negation of my own imperfection. But the argument from doubting, if valid, proves only that the idea of perfection must be simultaneous with the idea of imperfection, not that it must be prior. The principle that the positive is prior to the negative is worthless. The ability to use a predicate is not prior to, but identical with, the ability to use its negation. And the actual use of a negative predicate does not suppose the actual use of a positive one in a true predication. Geach has shown that we must reject the view that a negative predication needs to be backed by an affirmative one. "What positive predication," he asks, "justifies us in saying that pure water has no taste?" [4]

After his proof that the idea of God is not negative, Descartes attempts to show that it is not false. We noticed in the previous chapter the ambiguities involved in the notion of materially false ideas. In the present passage Descartes seems to trade on these ambiguities. He proves that his idea is true by saying that even if nothing in existence corresponds to it, it contains more objective reality than any other (AT VII, 46; HR I, 166). But this statement only shows that it is true in the sense in which "true" is equivalent to "genuine" or "real" or "positive" and in which true ideas are contrasted with negative ideas (e.g., AT VII, 54; HR I, 172). It does not show that it is true in the sense in which "true" is contrasted with "materially false," the sense in which an idea is true only if it is like that of which it is the idea (AT VII, 43; HR I, 164).

Descartes argues also that his idea of God is true on the grounds that it is clear and distinct. We may agree immediately that if an idea is clear and distinct then it is true in the sense of being nonnegative. We cannot yet agree, however, that clear and distinct ideas are true in the sense opposed to material falsehood; for that is something Descartes later proves by appeal to the veracity of God. The principle cannot be used, under pain of circularity, in proving the existence of the veracious God himself.

The clarity and distinctness of the idea is itself open to question. We have seen that it is not established by the original argument from doubting. "This idea is very clear and distinct," Descartes says, "since whatever I conceive clearly and distinctly that is real and true and involves some perfection, is in its entirety contained in this idea" (AT VII, 46; HR I, 166). But because the idea of A is clear and distinct and the idea of B is clear and distinct it by no means follows that the idea of A + B is clear and distinct. The idea of red and the idea of green are, or can be made, clear and distinct ideas (AT VIII, 32; HR I, 247); but the idea of something red and green all over is not at all clear and distinct. Perhaps red and green are not perfections; but then Descartes owes us an account of exactly what makes a property a perfection. Elsewhere he provides a better reason for regarding the idea of God as clear and distinct—

namely, the possibility of proving a priori nontrivial theorems about God (AT VII, 68; HR I, 182). But this is better considered in the following chapter.

Having established the existence in himself of a clear and distinct idea of God, Descartes inquires about its origin. His proof of God in the *Third Meditation* is a causal proof in that it is based on a principle of causality. It differs from other cosmological proofs of the existence of God in that the effect to which the causal principle is in the first instance applied is not any thing or event in the external world, but simply a thought in his own mind.

Descartes often states his causal principle in the blunt form "nothing comes from nothing," *ex nihilo nihil fit* (e.g., AT VII, 41, 135; HR I, 162; HR II, 35). After Hume, it is not possible to take this principle unquestioningly as a self-evident truth. Hume wrote:

> As all distinct ideas are separable from each other and as the ideas of cause and effect are evidently distinct, 'twill be easy for us to conceive any object to be non-existent this moment, and existent the next, without conjoining to it the distinct idea of a cause or productive principle . . . consequently the actual separation of these objects is so far possible, that it implies no contradiction nor absurdity.[5]

Descartes' contemporaries, without questioning the principle as radically as Hume, took exception to the way in which it was employed in the *Meditations*. Descartes gives as a more precise and general form of the principle the maxim "There must be at least as much reality in the efficient and total cause as in its effect."

This seems plausible in many cases; for instance, a

stove burning at less than 100°C will never heat water
to the boiling point. The second objectors produced a
counterexample: flies, plants, and other living things
were produced by the lifeless sun and rain and earth
(AT VII, 123; HR II, 25). Examples of evolution by
natural selection would nowadays provide more plausible counterinstances. Descartes in reply was suitably
skeptical about the spontaneous generation of flies; was
it certain that sun, rain, and earth were total and adequate causes? (AT VII, 134; HR II, 34.) He went on to
rebuke the objectors for drawing instances from the
material world, whose reality, in the strategy of the
Meditations, was still in suspense. This was unfair. As
Descartes himself remarked to Bourdin, a merely probable difficulty is sufficient to render a principle uncertain
(AT VII, 474; HR II, 277).

Other critics took exception to the application of
the causal principle to the objective realm. "In order
that an idea should contain some one objective reality
rather than another," wrote Descartes, "it must without
doubt derive it from some cause in which there is at
least as much formal reality as this idea contains of objective reality" (AT VII, 41; HR I, 163). "It needs no
cause," objected Caterus, "for its objective reality is a
mere name and nothing actual." No reason need be
given why a particular idea had one content rather than
another: "a boat is a boat, as Davus is Davus and not
Oedipus" (AT VII, 93; HR II, 2-3).

Caterus' criticisms seem mistaken. Descartes is right
that the content of an idea or picture, as well as the
formal reality of an idea or picture, calls for explanation.
If a man asks his wife for an explanation of a photo-

graph of her kissing the milkman, he is not going to be satisfied with even the fullest account of how a camera functions (cf. AT III, 567). We make causal inquiries within the objective realm whenever we raise questions of literary dependence, for example, when we ask whether Descartes invented the idea of the *cogito* or whether he took it from Augustine. Obviously it would be foolish to ask why the idea of God is the idea of God, but what is in question is not that, but how there comes to be an idea of God at all.

Most people would say that they acquired their idea of God from the teaching of their parents or the community in which they live. Critics pointed out that those who grew up in barbarous societies, such as the Hurons in Canada, lacked the idea (AT VII, 124; HR II, 26). Descartes replied that appeal to tradition merely postponed the question about the origin of the idea of God. If the idea could be invented by a human being, then I might have invented it myself; if it could not, then there remained the question whence it had come to my ancestors, however remote (AT VII, 135; HR II, 35).

"It may be the case," he said, "that one idea gives birth to another idea, but that cannot continue to be so indefinitely; for in the end we must reach an idea whose cause shall be so to speak an archetype in which the whole reality which is objectively in the ideas is contained formally." Why? Because it is of the nature of ideas that their ultimate causes have formal existence: by the light of nature I know that "ideas are in me like copies (*imagines*) which can fall short of the perfection of the objects from which they are derived, but cannot contain anything greater or more perfect" (AT VII, 42; HR I, 163). Some of my ideas contain properties that are in me formally (e.g., those of duration and thought), and others contain properties that are in me eminently (e.g., those of extension and motion); consequently, these ideas can have their origin in myself. But the idea of God contains properties that are not in me, nor in anything less than God, either formally or eminently; therefore, that idea must derive from an actually existing God (AT VII, 45; HR I, 165).

In this argument, the notion of "eminence" is obscure. Apparently, to have a property F eminently is not to have the property F but to have instead some grander property G. The admission that an idea of F may be derived from something that has F only eminently seems to destroy the argument that ideas must have a nonideal archetype because ideas are copies. If all ideas are copies, then what is in any idea objectively must be in its original formally; if some ideas contain properties that are not in their originals formally, then not all ideas are copies and no argument can be drawn from the copylike nature of an idea against the theory that ideas might derive from other ideas indefinitely.

Even if there is not an endless series of ideas producing ideas, might it not be possible for a human being to invent the idea of God by extrapolating from finite properties to be found in himself? Descartes seems both to admit and to reject this possibility. When he explained to Hobbes how we form the idea of God, he said, "Who is not aware of sometimes understanding? Everybody then has this content, the idea of understanding; and by indefinitely extending it, he forms the idea of God's understanding" (AT VII, 188; HR II, 73).

In the *Second Replies*, Descartes while agreeing with the objectors that there is in ourselves sufficient foundation on which to construct the idea of God, insisted that the very capacity for constructing such an idea could not exist in us unless there really is a God (AT VII, 133; HR II, 33). The *Third Meditation* concludes with an argument to bring this out: the proof Descartes offers that a being that has an idea of God must be created by God.

"From whom," he asks, "do I derive my existence?" He considers in turn the possibility that he derives it from himself, from his parents, from some other source less than God, and concludes that he derives it from God. Because of the principle *ex nihilo nihil fit* he does not consider the possibility that perhaps he has no cause but came into existence out of nothing.

The suggestion that his existence derives from himself divides into two hypotheses, according to whether his existence had a beginning or not. In considering the first hypothesis, Descartes does not argue, as we might expect, that in order to give himself existence he would have had to exist before he existed, which would be absurd. That is because he believed that even before he existed he was not absolutely nothing, and therefore his giving himself existence would not be a violation of the principle that nothing can come from nothing. This mysterious doctrine will be treated more fully in the next chapter.

Instead, Descartes argues that if he were himself the author of his being, he would have given himself various perfections, such as omniscience and omnipotence, which he lacks. This would be no more difficult than to give himself existence, since in giving himself existence he would be producing a substance, whereas in giving himself these attributes he would merely be endowing himself with accidents. This seems a strange argument. Parents are able to bring children into existence, but they cannot endow them with omniscience. To this Descartes could reply—in accordance with Catholic orthodoxy—that parents do not beget the souls of their children (AT VII, 50; HR I, 170). But even if parents beget only bodies, still they cannot endow these bodies with every perfection of strength and beauty that they might wish, and Descartes' principle still seems falsified. To this, it seems, Descartes could only reply that parents do not really beget bodies either. Bodies are only parts of matter; the production of a new human body is merely the division of matter in a new way. The parents merely "implant certain dispositions in that matter in which the self is deemed to exist" (ibid.). On Descartes' principles, then, neither thinking substances nor bodily substances can be produced by anyone but God. This conclusion was underlined by Descartes' disciple Malebranche.

The second hypothesis Descartes considers is the possibility that he always existed. This will not obviate the need for an author of his existence: ". . . for all the course of my life may be divided into an infinite number of parts, none of which is in any way dependent on the other; and thus from the fact that I was in existence a short time ago it does not follow that I must be in existence now, unless some cause at this instant, so to speak, produces me anew." This theory that one's life is built up out of instants, in the way in which movement in the cinema is built out of a series of stills, has had distinguished modern proponents. Several philosophers have thought that the life of a human being such as Socrates should be looked upon as a logical construction out of a set of time slices, Socrates at t, Socrates at t_1, Socrates at t_2, and so on. There are a number of difficulties about such a conception, which I will not discuss.[6] Even if we accept it, it seems that we need not grant Descartes his conclusion. For why may not each time slice be the cause of the existence of the next, dying phoenixlike in giving birth to its successor? There will be no violation of the principle that a cause must be as perfect as its effect; nothing can be imagined that more exactly equals in perfection a time slice of Descartes than an immediately preceding time slice of Descartes. Descartes counters this move by saying that if one momentary ego had the power of producing the next momentary ego, it would be conscious of this power. "For since I am nothing but a thinking thing, or at least since at the moment I am discussing in abstraction only that part of me which is a thinking thing, if any such power was in me, I should certainly be conscious of it" (AT VII, 49; HR I, 169). Here Descartes is falling into the error that we signaled in Chapter Four, of treating "I, qua known by me" as if it stood for some part of me. Because I, qua known by me, have no power to perpetuate myself, it by no means follows that I have not, unknown to myself, such a power.

Descartes next considers whether he may not have been caused by some being outside himself less than

God. Any such cause must, like himself, be a thinking thing, possessing the ideas of all the attributes of God. And concerning any such cause we can raise the question "Where did it come from?" "And it is perfectly manifest that in this there can be no regression into infinity, since what is in question is not so much the cause which formerly created me, as that which conserves me at the present time" (AT VII, 50; HR I, 169). As this passage suggests, if Descartes' argument for continuous creation can be refuted, he has no argument to show that he has not been produced by his parents, and they by their parents, and so on. For this would lead, not to an infinite regress of explanations that fail to explain, but simply to an endless series of causes, each of which is the effect of its predecessor. The notion of such a series has not been shown to be incoherent.[7]

Descartes concludes that he must have come from God and that the idea of God is innate in him, "like the mark of a workman imprinted on his work." Even if he is right that the idea of God must originate from God, he has provided no argument in the *Third Meditation* to show that this idea was not transmitted to him by God through society (AT VII, 51; HR I, 170).

By studying the idea of God, Descartes comes to the conclusion that "He cannot be a deceiver, since the light of nature teaches us that fraud and deception necessarily proceed from some defect." From this principle he later proves the validity of mathematics and the reality of the external world. Before considering these matters, we must turn to his other independent proof of the existence of God: the ontological argument.

SEVEN

THE ONTOLOGICAL ARGUMENT

I

In the *Discourse on Method* Descartes says:

> I saw quite clearly that, assuming a triangle, its three
> angles must be equal to two right angles; but for all
> that I saw nothing that assured me that there was
> any triangle in the real world. On the other hand,
> going back to an examination of my idea of a perfect
> being, I found that this included the existence of
> such a being; in the same way as the idea of a triangle
> includes the equality of its three angles to two right
> angles, or the idea of a sphere includes the equi-
> distance of all parts (of its surface) from the centre;
> or indeed in an even more evident way. Conse-
> quently it is at least as certain that God, the perfect
> being in question, is or exists, as any proof in geome-
> try can be. (AT VI, 36; HR I, 104)

Let us take the steps of this proof in turn. What is meant by "assuming a triangle" (*supposant une triangle*)? Does it mean "assuming some triangle exists"? Etienne Gilson glosses: "the supposition that a triangle be given, whether it exist really or not," and appeals to the Latin text: *si exempli causa supponamus dari aliquod triangulum*.[1] I believe that this is correct; but so far as this text goes, it looks as if we have two alternatives:

(1) If a triangle exists, it has its three angles equal to two right angles.
(2) Any triangle, whether it exists or not, has its three angles equal to two right angles.

We may notice that the difference between these formulations cannot be translated into Frege-Russell notation; and we may notice, too, as Descartes says, that neither contains any assurance "that there is any triangle in the real world."

Further light is thrown on Descartes' meaning by a passage in the *Fifth Meditation*.

When I imagine a triangle, it may be that no such figure exists anywhere outside my thought, and never has existed; but there certainly is its determinate nature, its essence, its form, which is unchangeable and eternal. This was not invented by me, and does not depend on my mind, as is clear from the following: various properties can be proved of this triangle, e.g. that its three angles are together equal to two right angles, that its greatest side subtends its greatest angle, and so on. (At VII, 64; HR I, 180)

He says (a little above) that this is an example of "things, which even if they perhaps exist nowhere outside me, cannot be said to be nothing."

This passage, by substituting for the phrase "to be in the world" of the *Discourse* the phrase "exist outside my thought," brings in by implicit contrast the notion of "existence in thought." Moreover, unlike the *Discourse* passage it distinguishes between the triangle, on the one hand, and the nature or essence or form of the triangle on the other. Further, it adds a more fortunate example of an eternal and immutable property of a triangle: even of non-Euclidean triangles it is true that the greatest side subtends the greatest angle.

It is clear, I think, that what Descartes means by a triangle existing in the world, or existing outside thought, is that there is in the world some body of triangular shape. Obviously, someone who is in doubt whether any body exists at all does not know whether, in this sense, any triangle exists in the world. But the supposition that no triangles exist in the world is not merely a part of Descartes' hyperbolical doubt. He believes the supposition to be true of the macroscopic world even after he provides the solution to his methodic doubts:

> I do not agree that these (geometric figures) have ever fallen under our senses, as everyone normally believes, because though there is no doubt that there could be in the world figures such as the geometers consider, I deny that there are any around us, unless perhaps they be so small that they make no impression on our senses; because they are for the most part made up of straight lines, and I do not think that

> any part of a line has touched our senses which was
> strictly straight.

and he appeals to the way straight lines look wavy under a magnifying glass (AT VII, 381; HR II, 227).

These passages make it likely that it is alternative
(2) and not (1) that Descartes has in mind. The theorem about the angles of a triangle is not meant to be
a counterfactual about what would be the case if there
were, as there are not, triangles existent in the world.
It is meant to be an actual statement about something
that can be a subject of predication even when there
are no triangles in existence. But a question arises: In
the absence of existent triangles, *what* is it that has the
properties ascribed by the theorems?

Hobbes raised this question in his fourteenth objection.

> If a triangle exists nowhere, I do not understand how
> it can have a nature; for what is nowhere, is not, and
> therefore has not a being or a nature . . . The truth
> of the proposition "a triangle is something having its
> three angles equal to two right angles" is everlasting.
> But the nature of a triangle is not everlasting; all
> triangles might cease to be.

Similarly, the proposition "Man is an animal" is true
forever because names are everlasting, but when the
human race ceases to be, human nature will be no
more. Hobbes' objection is wrapped up in his theory
that to predicate is to attach a second name to something; but the objection is independent of that theory.
Descartes replied, "Everybody is familiar with the distinction of essence and existence; and this talk about

names as being everlasting (instead of our having notions or ideas of eternal truths) has already been sufficiently refuted" (AT VII, 193; HR II, 76).

This reply is hardly adequate. But the following answer seems possible. What exists in no way, neither in the world nor in thought, can have no nature; but the triangle exists in thought and has a true and immutable nature that persists whether or not any triangles outside thought exist or cease to be.

Such, however, does not seem to be Descartes' view. In the *Meditations*, it appears to be things, not ideas, that have true and immutable natures. "I find in myself innumerable ideas of things which, even if they do not exist outside me, cannot be said to be nothing; and though they can be thought of by me more or less at will, they are not my inventions, but have their true and immutable natures" (AT VII, 64; HR I, 180).* It does not seem that we can say that for a triangle, *dari est cogitari*. For Descartes says that "it is not necessary for me ever to imagine any triangle; but whenever I choose to consider a rectilinear figure that has just three angles, I must ascribe to it properties from which it is rightly inferred that its three angles are not greater than two right angles" (AT VII, 67; HR I, 182). Now it has just been said—apropos of the idea of God—that thought imposes no necessity on things, but the necessity of the thing determines thought. Analogously, Descartes should say that this necessity of ascribing

---

* The Latin and French texts are both ambiguous as to whether it is the ideas, or the things, that have true and immutable natures; but it is clearly of *res*, and not of *ideae*, that Descartes says *"non tamen dici possunt nihil esse."*

certain properties to a triangle comes from the triangle
and not from thought. So we reach the conclusion that
what has the eternal and immutable nature is a triangle, and not the idea of a triangle; and we add that
this triangle, which has the provable properties, is given,
datur, whether or not Descartes or any other man has
an idea of a triangle. In reply to Hobbes, Descartes
must say that not only what exists in the world and not
only what exists in the mind, but also that which is
given, whether or not it exists and whether or not it is
thought of, has a nature.

If I am right, we have in Descartes' apparatus three
possible different states of affairs:

> *triangulus datur*
> *triangulus cogitatur*
> *triangulus existit*

That to which "*triangulus*" refers in each of these sentences is the same, though only if the second is true is
there an idea of a triangle, and only if the third is true
is there an actually existent triangle. This interpretation
can be confirmed by a close reading of the *Second Replies* (AT VII, 162; IIR II, 53) and the *Principles* (AT
VIII, 9–10; HR I, 225).[2]

Perhaps the fullest working out of the ontological
argument comes in the *First Replies* (AT VII, 115 ff.;
HR II, 19). The kernel of the argument is stated thus:
That which we clearly and distinctly understand to
belong to the true and immutable nature of anything,
its essence or form, can be truly affirmed of that thing.
This again cannot be the existent thing, for that would
involve a gross begging of the question when applied

to the nature of God. This major premise is not argued for by Descartes in this place, because he says it has already been agreed by the objector that whatever we clearly and distinctly perceive is true. Now strictly, there is a leap here: From this principle, plus the fact that we clearly and distinctly understand some property to belong to the true and immutable nature of something, it follows only that the property in question does belong to the true and immutable nature of the thing, not that it can be truly affirmed of it. But provided we take the thing to which the property belongs to be a not necessarily existent thing, then the leap is not a big one: it involves only the further principle that what has a nature has the properties that belong to the nature. But if we take it that properties can only be affirmed of existent things, the leap is fallacious; for something might belong to the nature of triangle and yet not be true of any triangle because no triangle existed.

A little further on Descartes says, "If I think of a triangle . . . then I shall truly affirm of the triangle all the things which I recognise to be contained in the idea of the triangle, as that its angles are equal to two right angles etc." Once again, the triangle of which this property is truly affirmed is not any existent triangle. But what is the relation between the *nature* of the not-necessarily-existent triangle and the *idea* of a triangle? It is not that every time I think of a triangle, I think of everything contained in the nature of the triangle. "Though I can think of a triangle while restricting my thought in such a manner that I do not think at all of its three angles being equal to two right angles, yet I cannot deny that attribute of it by any clear and distinct mental operation, i.e. rightly understanding what I say" (AT VII, 117; HR II, 20). So whatever belongs to the nature of a triangle is contained in the idea of a triangle; but not every time that I think of a triangle do I think of what is contained in the idea of a triangle (*ibid.*).

It seems to be true in general that whatever belongs to the nature of X is contained in the idea of X; but the converse is not true, that wherever we have an idea containing certain elements there is some nature composed of corresponding elements. The idea of a triangle is both simple and innate; others are composite and factitious. Some composite ideas, it seems, have natures corresponding to them. Take, for instance, the idea of a triangle inscribed in a square. It is not part of the nature of a triangle to be so inscribed, nor part of the nature of a square to contain such a triangle. Nonetheless, the composite figure itself has a true and immutable nature, and accordingly, certain properties are true of it, for example, that the area of the square cannot be less than double that of the inscribed triangle. But others do not. The idea, for instance, of a Hippogriff or winged horse is a composite and factitious idea (AT VII, 37; HR I, 159). This fact comes out in the control that the mind has over such ideas. "Those ideas which do not contain a true and immutable nature, but only a fictitious one put together by the mind, can be divided by the same mind, not merely by abstraction or restriction of thought but by a clear and distinct operation." What mind has put together, mind can put asunder. "For example, when I think of a winged horse . . . I easily understand that I can on the contrary think of a horse without wings"—not just think of a horse without thinking of his wings, but think of a horse without wings, clearly understanding what I'm thinking about. So here we have an idea which contains the property of being winged, plus the properties constituting the nature of horse; but there is no thing, existent or nonexistent, which has these properties as its nature (AT VII, 117; HR II, 20).

I do not think that Descartes makes clear what is supposed to be the difference between the winged horse and the triangle inscribed in the square. If I can think of a horse without wings, equally I can think of a triangle not inscribed in a square. If I cannot think of a triangle-in-the-square without certain properties, equally I cannot think of a winged horse without wings. Perhaps the difference is this. The properties of a winged horse are just the sum total of the properties of a horse and the properties of being winged plus the various combinations of these. But the proportion Descartes mentions as a property of a triangle inscribed in a square is not a property of a triangle as such, considered without reference to any square; nor is it a property of a square as such, considered without reference to any triangle. "I cannot think of a winged horse without wings" is true because I cannot think of a winged X without wings, no matter what X may be. "I cannot think of a triangle inscribed in an X which is more than half the area of the figure in which it is inscribed" is not true no matter what X may be. I am not sure exactly what Descartes' view was on this matter. Nor was Descartes. As Ernest Sosa has pointed out to me, Descartes both affirms and denies that a triangle inscribed in a square has a true and immutable essence (AT VII, 117; HR II, 20).

Descartes' views as I have expounded them bear a strong resemblance to those of Alexius Meinong. Just as Descartes distinguishes between "*datur*" and "*existere*" so Meinong makes a distinction between "*es gibt*" and "*sein*." For Descartes not only what exists has a nature but also what is given has a nature. Similarly, Meinong writes, "The figures with which geometry is concerned do not exist. Nevertheless their properties can be established." He called this the principle of the independence of *Sosein* from *Sein*. For Descartes it is not necessary that there should be an idea of X for a nonexistent X to be given and have properties. Similarly, Meinong wrote that "it is no more necessary to an object that it be presented (to the mind) in order not to exist than it is in order for it to exist." For Descartes there is something that is a triangle whether or not any triangle exists. Such a triangle is surely very like a Meinongian Pure Object, which "stands beyond being and nonbeing." [3]

Within the realm of being, Meinong makes a further distinction between subsistence (*Bestand*) and existence (*Existenz*). He gives as examples of things that subsist: similarities, differences, numbers, logical connections, and the existence of the antipodes. If two objects are similar, then there subsists a similarity between them. Roughly, subsistence appears to be the being of abstract objects, and existence appears to be the being of concrete objects. The corresponding distinction in Descartes would seem to be that between two sorts of being or *entitas*—namely, modal being (*entitas modalis*), which belongs to the attributes of things, and reality (*realitas*), which belongs to substances only. "Whatever is real can exist separately from any other subject; and whatever can exist thus separately is a substance" (AT VII, 434; HR II, 250; cf. AT III, 430; AT VII, 253, 364; HR II, 119, 215).

II

Thus far, we have been considering the first stage of Descartes' ontological argument, his statement that "assuming a triangle, its three angles must be equal to two right angles." We must now turn to his application of his principles. "Going back to an examination of my idea of a perfect Being, I found that this included the existence of such a being. Consequently, . . . it is . . . certain that God, the perfect being in question, is or exists." So the *Discourse*, arguing from the idea of God. The *Meditations* reaches the same conclusion from a consideration of the essence of God.

> I clearly see that existence can no more be separated from the essence of God than can its having three angles equal to two right angles be separated from the essence of a triangle, or the idea of a mountain from the idea of a valley; and so there is no less absurdity in thinking of a God (a supremely perfect being) who lacks existence than in thinking of a mountain without a valley. (AT VII, 66; HR I, 181)

(By a mountain without a valley, Descartes explained to Gibieuf, he meant an uphill slope without a downhill slope [III, 472].)

Gassendi, anticipating Kant, objected that existence should not be compared in this manner with a property.

Neither in God nor in anything else is existence a perfection, but rather that without which there are no perfections . . . Existence cannot be said to exist in a thing like a perfection; and if a thing lacks existence, then it is not just imperfect or lacking perfection; it is nothing at all. When you were listing the perfections of a triangle, you did not count existence, and you did not draw any conclusion about the existence of the triangle. Similarly, when listing the perfections of God, you should not have included existence, or drawn the conclusion that God exists, unless you want to beg the question. (AT VII, 323; HR II, 186)

Descartes replied:

I do not see what sort of thing you want existence to be, nor why it cannot be called a property just as much as omnipotence, provided that we use the word "property" for any attribute, or whatever can be predicated of a thing. (AT VII, 382; HR II, 228)

Clearly, he had missed the point of Gassendi's criticism, but Gassendi's remarks, in turn, were based on a mis-understanding. He did not realize that for Descartes the subject of the sentence "God exists" was a pure object, beyond being and nonbeing. A pure object can have properties whether or not it exists; but if we are in-quiring about its properties, one of the most interesting questions we can ask is "Does it exist or not?" In making predications of a pure object we are not begging the question of its existence; and when Descartes con-cludes "God exists" from the premise "God is supremely perfect," he is drawing his conclusion not from the oc-currence of the word "God" in the subject place of his premise, but from the way in which he believes that the predicate "exists" is included in the predicate "is supremely perfect." The objection "existence is not a predicate" amounts to this: "exists" cannot be a predicate because if it is false of any subject then there is no such subject for it to be false of. But this objection has no force unless there is an independent argument to show that Meinongian pure objects are incoherent. For even if there is no God, so that "God exists" is false, there is always the appropriate pure object to sustain the false predicate.

Hume denied that existence could form part of the content of an idea: "The idea of existence is nothing different from the idea of any object, and when after the simple conception of any thing we would conceive it as existent, we in reality make no addition or alteration on our first idea." [4] The idea of an existent X is the same as the idea of an X. To some extent Descartes anticipated this line of objection. "We never think of things without thinking of them as existents," he wrote (AT VII, 117; HR II, 20). All ideas, therefore, in a sense, contain existence (AT VII, 166; HR II, 57). But whereas the ideas of other things contain possible existence, the idea of God contains necessary existence. The mind sees that in the idea of a supremely perfect being "there is contained existence—not merely possible and contingent existence, as in the ideas of all other things which it distinctly perceives, but altogether necessary and eternal existence" (AT VII, 116; HR II, 19; AT VIII, 10; HR I, 10).

Descartes' meaning seems to be this. Take the defining properties of any entity: let "F" represent a pred-

icate term signifying those properties. If we can clearly
and distinctly conceive of an entity that is F, then we
know that it is *possible* for there to exist an entity that
is F. In the case of God, however, we can draw a
stronger conclusion. Where the properties in question
are those that define God, we know that it is *necessary*
for an entity that is F to exist. "We conceive clearly that
actual existence is necessarily and always conjoint with
the other attributes of God" (AT VII, 116; HR II, 19).

This is proved by Descartes in two distinct man-
ners. Generally, he argues that since God is perfect and
existence is a perfection, it follows necessarily that God
exists (AT VII, 66; HR I, 181; AT VII, 166; HR II, 57;
AT VI, 36; HR I, 104). In the *First Replies*, it is not
from God's perfection, but from His omnipotence that
the argument is drawn.

> Because we cannot think of God's omnipotence as
> being possible, without at the same time, and by
> taking heed of His immeasurable power, acknowledg-
> ing that He can exist by His own might, we hence
> conclude that He really exists and has existed from all
> eternity; for the light of nature makes it most plain
> that what can exist by its own power always exists.
> (AT VII, 119; HR II, 21)

This last passage creates a peculiar mental discom-
fort; at least, we feel, there must be some important
premises suppressed. Descartes himself was not altogether happy about the argument. At first he had
written thus: "We cannot think of His existence as
being possible without at the same time thinking that
there must be possible some power by means of which

he exists; and that power cannot be conceived to be in anything else than in that same supremely powerful being; and so we conclude that He can exist by His own might." But before these words went to the printer, he asked Mersenne to cancel them so that the curious could not decipher them, in case anybody attacked the author "in the place which he himself judged to be the weakest" (AT III, 330).

The stages of the argument seem to be as follows:

(1) God's existence is possible.

This is shown because we have a clear and distinct idea of God (AT VII, 119); and this in turn is proved because "whatever I clearly and distinctly perceive, which is real and true and involves some perfection is all contained in [the idea of God]" (AT VII, 46; HR I, 166). This is the part of the argument Leibniz thought deficient. It needed to be proved, he said, that all perfections were compatible with each other; otherwise the idea of an all-perfect being would imply a contradiction. Leibniz himself was prepared to offer such a proof, which convinced Spinoza but has not satisfied modern critics.[5]

(2) God is by definition all-powerful and independent.

This is said in the *Third Meditation* (AT VII, 45 ff.). It followed from this, Descartes thought, that if He can exist at all He can exist by his own power. But we know that God can exist. Therefore:

(3) God can exist by His own power.
(4) What can exist by its own power, does exist.

It is this step that at first seems most in need of justification. I suggest that there are two suppressed premises: (a) If you can do something by your own power and you do not do it, then it can only be because you do not want to do it; and (b) everything wants to exist. Now (a) is plausible enough, and is commonly accepted when it is appealed to in a famous formulation of the problem of evil ("If God can prevent evils, and does not prevent them, then He must not want to prevent them"). Premise (b) sounds odd to us, but in fact *omnia appetunt esse* was a scholastic commonplace. Now (a) and (b) together yield (4), and (3) and (4) together give:

(5) God exists.

One misgiving we may feel here concerns the application of (b) to pure objects. We may be prepared to go so far with Descartes and Meinong as to admit that nonexistent entities can have natures and properties, but surely they cannot have *desires*. This misgiving seems unfounded. If we are to make predications of the nonexistent at all, among the predications we must make will be some that involve desires. For instance, we shall have to say that satyrs (though no satyrs exist) have the libidinous appetites ascribed to them by classical authorities. A nonlibidinous satyr would not be a satyr at all.

The premises from which Descartes here derives the existence of God have always been true; therefore he concludes not only that God exists, but that He has existed from all eternity. "For the light of nature makes it most plain that what can exist by its own power always exists."

The light of nature can do so, I contend, only if it shows us also that everything desires existence. *"Omnia appetunt esse"* is explicitly supplied by Aquinas as a suppressed premise to rescue from fallacy an argument of Aristotle's that purported to show that whatever can corrupt sometimes does corrupt, so that any everlasting being must be a necessary being.[6] When scholastics spoke of "necessary being" they did not mean a being whose existence was a necessary truth; they meant a being that, in the order of nature, could not cease to exist. For medieval Aristotelians the stars were necessary beings in this sense. Their existence was not a necessary truth; it was contingent on the will of God, Who might never have created. But they were naturally indestructible and could cease to exist only being annihilated by their creator. Obviously, something whose existence was a logically necessary truth, would *a fortiori* be necessary in the scholastic sense; but the converse does not hold.

It is important to underline this distinction. A recent revival of the ontological argument by Norman Malcolm runs as follows:

> If God, a being greater than which cannot be conceived, does not exist, then He cannot come into existence . . . Since He cannot come into existence, if He does not exist his existence is impossible. If He does exist, He cannot have come into existence . . . nor can He cease to exist, for nothing could cause Him to cease to exist nor could it just happen that He ceased to exist. So if God exists, His existence is necessary. Thus God's existence is either impossible or necessary. It can be the former only if the

concept of such a being is self-contradictory or in some way logically absurd. Assuming that this is not so, it follows that He necessarily exists.[7]

There is a fallacy in this argument: "impossible" is being used in two senses. In one sense it is contrasted with the modern notion of logical necessity; in the other it is contrasted with the Aristotelian notion of necessary being. In the first sense it means "involving the violation of a logical truth"; in the second it means "incapable of being brought into or put out of existence." The statement "If God does not exist His existence is impossible" may be true in the sense that if God does not exist He cannot be brought into existence, without being true in the sense that if God does not exist, the statement "God exists" must involve the violation of a logical truth. But it must be true in the latter sense if the argument is to work.

Now it might seem that an analogous fallacy is being committed by Descartes when he argues that if God can exist at all, He can exist by His own power. For does not the first "can" refer to logical possibility, whereas the second "can" relates to powers residing in natural agents? I think, in fact, that Descartes' argument does not contain this fallacy, though it moves rather too fast. Premise (1) above certainly only shows that it is logically possible for God to exist, not that God has any power to exist. That God has the power to exist follows not from premise (1), but from the different premise that God is all-powerful: He can do everything, including exist. That God can exist *by His own power* follows from this, plus the premise that God is independent, that is, that He can do whatever He can do without help from anything else. That this is the line of Descartes' thought is, I think, shown by the passage he ordered Mersenne to cancel, though we may well sympathize with his despairing of presenting it in a clear and plausible manner.

Certainly, Descartes was aware of the possibility of the fallacious argument recorded above, and he pointed out the fallacy. In the *Second Replies* he discusses the argument "If it is not self-contradictory for God to exist, then it is certain that He exists; but it is not self-contradictory for Him to exist; *ergo* . . . " This argument, he says, is a sophism.

> For in the major the word "self-contradictory" has reference to the concept of a cause from which God would derive existence; in the minor, however, it refers only to the concept of the divine existence and nature. This is clear from the following. If the major is denied, it is proved as follows: if God does not yet exist, it is self-contradictory for Him to exist, because there cannot be any cause sufficient to produce Him; but it is not self-contradictory for Him to exist, *ergo* . . . But if the minor is denied, we shall have to say that is not self-contradictory, in the formal concept of which there is nothing which involves a contradiction; but in the formal concept of the divine existence or nature there is nothing which involves a contradiction, *ergo* . . . And these two are very different. (AT VII, 151; HR II, 46)

Descartes' God exists necessarily in the sense that "God exists" is a necessary truth.

It seems to me that if we give Descartes his Meinongian assumptions, there is nothing fallacious in his argument. This makes it the more extraordinary that Meinong himself did not accept the ontological argument. When he said that objects as such were beyond being and not being, Meinong was careful to add qualifications.

> This is not to say, of course, that an Object can neither be nor not be. Nor is it to say that the question, whether or not the object has being, is purely accidental to the nature of every Object. An absurd Object such as a round square carries in itself the guarantee of its own non-being in every sense; an ideal Object, such as diversity, carries in itself the guarantee of its own non-existence.

If this is so, one might ask Meinong, why cannot there be an object that carries in itself the guarantee of its own existence?

Russell, reviewing Meinong in 1905, claimed that he could not in consistency reject the ontological proof.

> If the round square is round and square the existent round square is existent and round and square. Thus something round and square exists although everything round and square is impossible. This ontological argument cannot be avoided by Kant's device of saying that existence is not a predicate. For [the Meinongians] admit that "existing" applies when and only when being "actual" applies, and that the latter is a *sosein*. Thus we cannot escape the consequence that the "existent God" both exists and is God, and it is hard to see how it can be maintained . . . that this has no bearing on the question whether God exists.[8]

Meinong could only reply that though God was existent, to be existent and to exist were not the same. Russell was surely right to be dissatisfied with such a reply.

More consistent than Meinong, Descartes accepted the ontological argument; more cautious than Meinong, he is not vulnerable to Russell's argument about the round square. It is customary to dismiss Meinongian pure objects with a high-handed reference to their "oddity," or by an appeal for "a robust sense of reality." Descartes would have regarded such a feeling for reality as a mere prejudice. The objections that such objects involve violations of the principle of noncontradiction are more serious. The round square, for instance, is both square (by definition) and not square (since whatever is round is not square).

Descartes could reply that this contradiction was the result, not of admitting pure objects, but of admitting impossible entities among them. Though Meinong did this, Descartes never did. He wrote, "In the concept of every thing there is contained either possible or necessary existence" (AT VIII, 2a, 60); what cannot exist, therefore, is no thing. "Possible existence," he wrote, "is a perfection in the idea of a triangle, just as necessary existence is a perfection in the idea of God; it is this which makes it superior to the ideas of those chimeras whose existence is regarded as nil (*nulla*)" (AT VIII, 383). Descartes would not have been trapped by the argument that if a round circle is impossible, then there must *be* something (viz., the round circle) to be impossible. "All self-contradiction (*implicantia*) or impossibility," he wrote, "arises in our conception, which mistakenly joins together ideas which clash with each other. It cannot be situated in anything outside the mind, because if something is outside the mind, then *eo ipso* it is not self-contradictory, but possible" (AT VII, 152; HR II, 46).

Descartes has an answer, too, to another argument suggested by Russell; namely, that if existence is a predicate, then we can conceive an existent golden mountain, and this must in its turn exist. He appeals to the distinction between true and immutable essences on the one hand and fictitious essences on the other. Let E be an essence that can be defined by the predicates F and G, so that a thing has F, if and only if it is both F and G. If F is part of the true and immutable essence of E, it is impossible for us to conceive of a G that is not F. If, on the other hand, we can conceive of a G that is not F, then, even though we can make up the notion of a G that is F, this will be a fictional essence and not an immutable essence. If we replace "F" by "winged" and "G" by "horse," then we have one of Descartes' favorite examples:

> . . . when I think of a winged horse, or of a lion actually existing, or of a triangle inscribed in a square, I easily understand that I can on the contrary think of a horse without wings, of a lion as not existing and of a triangle apart from a square, and so forth, and that hence these things have no true and immutable essence. (AT VII, 117; HR I, 20)

An existent golden mountain, then, does not have a true and immutable essence, and therefore no conclusion can be drawn about its existence. God, unlike the existent golden mountain, is no fiction, because we can prove a priori that what has the properties of God also has existence, though we cannot prove a priori that what has the properties of a golden mountain also has existence. Nonetheless, if Descartes is to avoid the conclusion that the existent golden mountain exists, it seems that he must deny that there is any such thing as the existent golden mountain; he must exclude it from the realm of pure objects. I do not know of any place where he explicitly does so, but it is compatible with all the texts known to me. In conclusion, we may say that Descartes' argument is most intelligible if we regard him as admitting, with Meinong, that there is a status of pure objecthood, beyond being and nonbeing, but, unlike Meinong, denying this status to impossible and fictional entities and restricting it to those entities that have true and immutable essences, that is, those about which nontrivial truths can be proved a priori or whose component properties are necessarily linked.

The most serious—indeed the insurmountable—objection to Meinongian pure objects is that it is impossible to provide any criterion of identity for them. If something is to be a subject of which we can make predications, it is essential that it shall be possible to tell in what circumstances two predications are made of *that same subject*. Otherwise we shall never be able to apply the principle that contradictory predications should not be made of the same subject. We have various complicated criteria by which we decide whether two statements are being made about the same actual man; by what criteria can we decide whether two statements are being made about the same *possible* man? The difficulties are entertainingly brought out in a famous paragraph by W. V. O. Quine.

Take, for instance, the possible fat man in that doorway; and again, the possible bald man in that doorway. Are they the same possible man, or two possible men? How do we decide? How many possible men are there in that doorway? Are there more possible thin ones than fat ones? How many of them are alike? Are no *two* possible things alike? Is this the same as saying that it is impossible for two things to be alike? Or, finally, is the concept of identity simply inapplicable to unactualised possibles? But what sense can be found in talking of entities which cannot meaningfully be said to be identical with themselves and distinct from one another? [9]

These objections, I think, make untenable the notion of Meinongian pure objects. We may with gratitude accept the alternative method of dealing with the nonexistent offered us, with the aid of quantifiers, by Frege and Russell. But it is perhaps worth remarking that when the pure object in question is God, then the difficulties about identification appear less palpable. For, in the nature of the case, only one omnipotent and all-perfect being is possible; so that we do not feel constrained to put to Descartes the question "Which God are you proving the existence of?" (Cf. AT VII, 68; HR I, 182.)

I shall not pursue these difficulties further here, but I wish to conclude this chapter by drawing attention to a major difficulty internal to Descartes' own system. If the ontological argument is not to be a great *petitio principii*, it is essential that it should be possible to prove properties of the problematically existent. It must be possible, at least in some cases, to be sure that X is F without being sure that X exists. But if that is so, then what becomes of *"cogito ergo sum"*? I have argued that it is an essential step in the *cogito* that every attribute must belong to a substance; "in order to think, one must exist" is just a particular case of this principle (AT VIII, 8; HR I, 223). But what right has Descartes to assume that the substance, of which his thought is an attribute, exists? If I can be sure that a triangle has its three angles equal to two right angles without being sure that any triangle exists, why can I not be sure that *ego cogito* without being sure that *ego existo*? On the other hand, if I can argue: "I am thinking, therefore I am," why can I not argue: "The triangle has three angles equal to two right angles, therefore the triangle exists"?

Perhaps I was incautious in saying that "in order to think one must exist" is a particular example of the principle that attributes cannot be attributes of nothing. Because "not to be nothing" and "to exist" are not synonyms, does not Descartes speak of the ideas of "things which even if they perhaps exist nowhere outside myself, cannot be said to be nothing"? (AT VII, 63; HR I, 179.) But if I was incautious, so is Descartes: In the *Second Meditation* he uses the two expressions as if they were synonymous. "Without doubt I exist even if he deceives me, and let him deceive me as much as he will, he can never cause me to be nothing so long as I think that I am something" (AT VII, 25; HR I, 150).

Descartes says that his system rests on two principles, his own existence and God's existence. If my account is right, he cannot have both these principles in quite the way he wants them. If what does not exist can have properties, then he can perhaps prove God's existence, but he cannot prove his own. If what does not exist cannot have properties, he can perhaps prove his own existence, but he cannot prove God's existence from God's essence without begging the question. The *cogito* and the ontological argument cannot both be valid.

EIGHT

REASON
AND
INTUITION

In the *First Meditation* Descartes questioned the testimony of the senses and then the operations of mathematics. Having established to his own satisfaction the existence of God, he was ready to reverse his earlier skepticism. The doubt engendered by the supposition of an omnipotent deceiver is to be laid to rest by the discovery of the veracious creator. "Certainty in knowledge is impossible," he said in the *Principles*, "until the mind has come to know the author of its being" (AT VIII, 10; HR I, 224).

The order in which the skeptical questions are answered reverses that in which they were raised. The last truths to be shaken are the first to be restored. These are called in the *Principles* "the demonstrations of mathematics and its principles." In the course of validating mathematics, however, Descartes discusses several propositions that seem to belong rather to logic or metaphysics. The establishment of the certainty of mathematics takes place in the *Third*, *Fourth*, and *Fifth Meditations*.

This process is sometimes called "the validation of reason." Such a description may suggest that in Descartes' system there is a single rational faculty whose function it is to understand, infer, and affirm the truths of a priori disciplines such as logic and arithmetic. This suggestion raises a problem. The construction of philosophical arguments would presumably be one of the exercises of such a faculty. If so, how can Descartes undertake to show by philosophical argument that the right use of reason leads to truth? How can one make use of a faculty in order to prove that faculty trustworthy? If the faculty is untrustworthy, then its own proof that it is trustworthy is worthless. One might as well call a witness in a court of law to testify to his own veracity.

In fact, Descartes does not speak of "reason" (*ratio*) in this context, and in his system there is no one faculty with all the functions listed above. He speaks of the mind (*mens, esprit*), of the understanding (*intellectus, entendement*), and of the will (*voluntas, volonté*). The mind, considered as a faculty, is the capacity for having thoughts of all kinds, including emotions and sense perceptions (AT VII, 173–175; HR II, 62–64). The understanding is the ability to have clear and distinct perceptions. The will is the ability to accept and reject, and in particular the ability to affirm and deny, to make positive and negative judgments. Thus the mind, the capacity for thought, includes the understanding and the will, which are the faculties or abilities to have particular kinds of thoughts (AT VIII, 17; HR I, 232).

None of these three corresponds to the faculty of "reason" described above. The mind includes the ability to see and hear: these are senses whose limited veracity is not established until the *Sixth Meditation*. The understanding has as one of its exercises the clear and distinct perception of a piece of wax (AT VII, 32; HR I, 155), an activity that seems to lie outside the field of logic and mathematics. On the other hand, a judgment within that field—even the judgment that two and three make five—is an exercise not of the understanding but of the will. "By the understanding alone I do not affirm or deny anything; I merely conceive the ideas of things as to which I can form a judgement" (AT VII, 56; HR I, 174). For Descartes, therefore, there is no one faculty whose function is to understand, infer, and affirm a priori truths.

Scholastic philosophers sometimes contrasted *ratio* with *intellectus*. By the latter they meant the grasping of concepts and the intuition of self-evident truths; by the former they meant the reaching of conclusions by reasoning.[1] Descartes sometimes uses words corresponding to "reason" to mark this distinction (e.g., AT V, 1, 6–8). In the third of the *Rules* he distinguishes between intuition and deduction. Some propositions are so simple that their truth can be seen in a single mental glance. We can intuit in this manner, for instance, that a triangle has three sides, and that two and two make four. Moreover, we can intuit not only single propositions but also the fact that one proposition follows from others. Thus we see that "$2 + 2 = 3 + 1$" follows from "$2 + 2 = 4$" and "$3 + 1 = 4$." Other propositions, however, neither are self-evident, nor do they follow with immediate self-evidence from self-evident principles. Such propositions may be known by deduction if they are proved by a succession of self-evident steps. Thus, I may be able to intuit that p, and I may be able to intuit that if p then q, and that if q then r. In such a case I may be certain that r without being able to intuit it. "It is in the same way," Descartes explains, "that we know the last link of a chain is connected with the first, even though we do not view in a single glance all the intermediate links on which the connection depends; we need only to have gone through the links in succession and to remember that from the first to the last each is joined to the next" (AT X, 370; HR I, 8).

In Descartes' methodic doubt, both intuited and deduced truths are called in question, though not in the same manner. In the *Meditations* and the *Principles* Descartes rarely uses the word "intuition." "Clear and distinct perception," an expression he uses frequently, cannot be regarded as a synonym for "intuition" since the conclusions of deductions may be clearly and distinctly perceived no less than self-evident truths (e.g., AT VII, 69; HR I, 184). But the examples Descartes gives to illustrate his doubt in the *First Meditation* are almost exactly the same as the examples he gave of intuited truths in the *Rules*. "May not God make me go wrong, whenever I add two to three, or count the sides of a square, or do any simpler thing that might be imagined?" (AT VII, 21; HR I, 147.) It seems clear from the beginning, therefore, that Descartes is in some way questioning mathematical intuition as well as mathematical proof.

In the *Rules*, intuition is said to be produced "by the light of reason alone." Similarly, we hear much in the *Meditations* and *Principles* of truths that are "known by the natural light in our souls" (e.g., AT VII, 38–44; HR I, 160–165; AT VIII, 8; HR I, 223). Among things said to be shown by the natural light are the following propositions:

> From the fact that I doubt, I can conclude that I exist. (AT VII, 38; HR I, 160)
> There must be at least as much reality in the efficient and total cause as in its effect. (AT VII, 40; HR I, 162)
> Fraud and deception necessarily proceed from some defect. (AT VII, 52; HR I, 171)
> What is done cannot be undone. (AT VII, 82; HR I, 193)
> Nothing can be the cause of nothing. (AT VIII, 11; HR I, 226)

As these examples show, principles said to be known by natural light are almost always metaphysical theses rather than mathematical axioms.

Some of the principles of natural light are also described in other terms. In the *Second Replies*, Descartes speaks of propositions that are "self-evident" (*per se notae*). He gives as examples: "the same thing cannot both be and not be," "nothing cannot be the efficient cause of anything," "two is even and three is odd" (AT VII, 62–63; HR II, 54–55). In the *Principles* he says:

I distinguish all the objects of our knowledge into two kinds: first, things which have existence; second, eternal truths which have no existence outside our thought. . . . When we apprehend that it is impossible that anything should be formed of nothing, the proposition "*ex nihilo nihil fit*" is not to be considered as an existing thing, or the mode of a thing, but as a certain eternal truth which has its seat in our mind, and is a common notion or axiom. Of the same nature are the following: "It is impossible that the same thing can be and not be at the same time" and "what has been done cannot be undone" and "he who thinks must exist while he thinks" and very many other propositions. (AT VIII, 23–24; HR I, 238–239)

Elsewhere in the same book he gives examples of "common notions": one is "if equals are added to equals, the result is equal" (AT VIII, 9; HR I, 224). "In order to think one must exist," he says, "is a notion of the simplest possible kind which of itself gives no knowledge of anything that exists" (AT VIII, 8; HR I, 222). This recalls the "simple notions" of the *Rules*, which include not only concepts such as that of *unity* and *duration* but also propositions such as "things that are the same as a third thing are the same as one another" (AT X, 419; HR I, 41). In the *Second Replies* Descartes gives a list of metaphysical principles including most of the ones already mentioned, which he names "Axioms or Common Notions," while admitting that some of them are perhaps better called theorems (AT VII, 164; HR, II, 55).

Descartes uses, then, at least six different expressions with closely related significance: "principles of natural light," "self-evident propositions," "eternal truths," "axioms," "common notions," "simple notions." The expression "eternal truth" in the *Principles* is not a synonym of "axiom," as Descartes told Burman it was (AT V, 167). If it were, he could not consistently have divided all possible objects of knowledge into things and eternal truths without denying that we could know any nonaxiomatic a priori truths. In his correspondence, one example Descartes gives of an eternal truth is "all the radii of a circle are equal," which seems as axiomatic as the truth that a triangle has three sides (AT I, 152). Elsewhere he writes as if all mathematical truths were eternal (AT I, 144), as indeed they are in the sense that they do not change their truth values in the way that a particular proposition such as "I am writing" does. Indeed the eternal truths probably include physical truths such as the laws of motion that Descartes tried to derive from a priori premises such as the immutability of God. For the eternal truths tell the essence of creatures (AT I, 151), but truths concerning the essence of physical bodies concern motion as well as geometrical matters.

What of the other five expressions? Are they synonymous? Or, if not synonymous, do they at least coincide in extension, so that each marks out one and the same class of propositions? The expressions do seem to be used interchangeably, but we seem to face a contradiction in Descartes' teaching: We are told that what is taught by natural light is indubitable, while it is possible for axioms and common notions to be doubted. Thus we read in the *Third Meditation*: "I cannot doubt that which the natural light causes me to believe to be true" (AT VII, 38; HR I, 160). In the

Principles we are told, with regard to the common notions, that "We cannot fail to know them when the occasion presents itself for thinking of them" (AT VII, 24; HR I, 239). But Descartes adds, *"if* we have no prejudices to blind us," and goes on to say that the common notions are not all equally evident to all men, since some are prevented from perceiving them by their prejudices (*ibid.*). But if a prejudiced man can think of an axiom without seeing it to be true, then he can doubt it and so the axiom must be dubitable.

The contradiction is only apparent. Instead of asking of a particular proposition whether it is dubitable or indubitable we should ask *when* it can be doubted, at what stage of one's philosophical progress it can be called into question. In the *Seventh Replies* Descartes rebuked Bourdin because "throughout he treats doubtfulness and certainty not as relations of our thought to its objects, but as properties of its objects inhering in them forever" (AT VII, 475; HR II, 276). Once something has been shown to me by natural light, Descartes says, I cannot doubt it; but another person who sees less clearly may doubt the very same proposition. It is not that one man has greater power of understanding than another, nor that there are any axioms incapable of being perceived by everyone; it is just that one man may be freer than another from prejudices, and a single man may at one time be blinded by prejudices from which he is later freed (AT VII, 477; HR II, 279).

There are, however, some axioms that no one can doubt at any stage of his life. Among the clear perceptions of the intellect, we are told in the *Second Replies:*

. . . there are some so evident and at the same time
so simple, that we cannot think of them without
believing them to be true: e.g. that I exist while I
think, and that what is once done cannot be undone,
and other similar truths, about which we clearly
possess this certainty. For we cannot doubt them
unless we think of them; and we cannot think of
them without at the same time believing them to be
true; i.e. we can never doubt them. (AT VII, 125;
HR II, 42)

There is then, a class of specially indubitable axioms—
axioms indubitable even by the prejudiced. But this
class may well be smaller than the class of axioms that
has been shown by natural light to a particular individual at a particular stage. A *fortiori*, it is smaller
than the class of axioms that *can* be shown by natural
light to anybody at any stage. The axioms Descartes
sets out in his geometrical statement of his system are
not among those that are indubitable, even to the unprejudiced. It does not suffice to read them in order to
see their truth; meditation is needed to remove the ob-
scuring effects of prejudice. Descartes advises the reader
to rehearse the self-evident propositions that he does
possess (e.g., the principles of noncontradiction and
causality) and thus employ in its purity "that clarity of
understanding that nature has implanted in them."
Thus, he says, the truth of his axioms will become
evident (AT VII, 162; HR II, 54). Things that appear
self-evident to the unprejudiced may need proof to the
prejudiced (AT VII, 164; HR II, 55). We are reminded
of the passage in the *Rules* where Descartes said that
"when propositions are direct conclusions from first

principles, they may be said to be known by intuition or by deduction, according to different ways of looking at them" (AT X, 370; HR I, 8).

It is important to note that even in the simplest cases, where a proposition cannot be thought of without being believed, we must distinguish clear and distinct perception, which is an act of the understanding, from belief, which is not. The propositions are so evident that we cannot help believing them, that is, affirming them to be true; but affirmation, since it is a judgment, is an act not of the understanding but of the will. Thus Descartes says in the *Fourth Meditation*:

> . . . during these last few days I have been considering whether anything in the world exists, and have observed that, from my examining of the question, it follows necessarily that I exist. I could not but judge to be true what I so clearly understood to be true; not because I was compelled to do so by any external cause, but because the great illumination of my understanding was followed by a great inclination of the will. (AT VII, 59; HR I, 176)

Though there are some axioms that no one can ever doubt, it does not seem that there are any axioms that everyone clearly knows. Indeed, in the *Principles*, we are told that "there are a number of people who throughout all their lives perceive nothing so correctly as to be capable of judging of it properly" (AT VIII, 21; HR I, 237). Since an axiom such as "What's done cannot be undone" cannot be doubted once it is thought of, and since anything can be doubted unless it is clearly and distinctly perceived (AT VIII, 6; HR I,

221), we seem to be left with the conclusion that those who never clearly and distinctly perceive anything can never even have had the thought "What's done cannot be undone." But in the *Seventh Replies* the same point is made with a qualification. Before going through the discipline of Cartesian doubt, we are there told, scarcely anyone perceives anything clearly, "at least with the clearness required for metaphysical certainty" (AT VII, 476; HR II, 279).

Metaphysical certainty is the certainty that resists even metaphysical doubt, and the nature of metaphysical doubt is explained most fully in a crucial passage of the *Third Meditation*.

When I was considering some very simple and very easy point in arithmetic or geometry, e.g. that two and three together make five, did I perceive this clearly enough to assert its truth? My only reason for judging afterwards that it was possible to doubt these things was that it occurred to me that perhaps some God could have given me such a nature that I was deceived even about what seemed most obvious. Now whenever the preconceived view that there is a supremely powerful God occurs to me, I am forced to admit that He could easily, if He wishes, make me go wrong even in the things which I believe I know most clearly. But whenever I turn to the things themselves which I think I perceive very clearly, I am so convinced by them that I cannot help exclaiming "Let who can deceive me, he can never bring it about that I am nothing while I think I am something, nor that it should ever be true that I have never existed, since it is now true that I exist, nor even that two and three together should make more or less than five, or other such things in which I see a manifest contradiction." . . . The argument from the possibility of a divine deceiver [is] a very slight —so to say a metaphysical—reason for doubting.

But to remove it, Descartes must show that there is a God who cannot deceive; "without knowing this I seem unable to be quite certain of anything else" (AT VII, 36; HR I, 158).

This passage has puzzled people because it looks as if Descartes is saying both that he can and that he cannot doubt that two and three make five. But the passage is self-consistent, though it needs careful attention. Notice first that two of the things he says that no one however powerful could bring about—namely, that I am nothing while I think I am something and that it should ever be true that I have never existed, since it is now true that I exist—are the counterparts of the two axioms ("I exist while I think"; "what is done cannot be undone") that Descartes gives as instances of propositions that could not be thought of without being believed. Thus, in this passage Descartes is considering not remote mathematical conclusions but those propositions he regarded as the most indubitable of all.

Second, notice that the passage suggests a distinction between a first-order doubt and a second-order doubt. Take the proposition "What's done cannot be undone." If I explicitly think of this proposition, Descartes says, I cannot at that moment doubt it, that is, I cannot help judging that it is true. However, though I cannot doubt this proposition while my mind's eye is on it, I can, as it were, turn away from it and doubt it in a roundabout manner. I can refer to it under some general heading, such as "what seems to me most obvious"; and I can raise the whole question whether everything that seems to me most obvious may not in fact be false. I cannot, while explicitly thinking of it, believe it to be false or even suspend judgment about its truth. But until I know that I was made by a veracious God, I can wonder whether my whole intellectual faculty may not be radically deceptive—including that feature of it that is its inability to entertain first-order doubt about metaphysical axioms of this kind. The axioms are thus generically doubtful while severally indubitable. While in doubt about the author of my nature, I do not know whether the light of nature is a true light or a false light. This second-order doubt is the metaphysical doubt that cannot be removed except by proving the existence of a veracious God.

In the passages we considered earlier in which Descartes spoke of certain axioms as being indubitable, we must take him to have been speaking of the possibility of first-order doubt. For his examples in the *Third Meditation* make clear that no axioms are immune to second-order doubt. First-order indubitability is not considered by Descartes as being, by itself, a guarantee of truth; still less does he use "indubitable" as equivalent to "true." The second-order doubt is precisely the question whether first-order indubitability is compatible with falsehood. God's truthfulness resolves the second-order doubt by showing that what is indubitable is true.[2]

When Descartes says we *cannot* doubt simple axioms, he is not yet saying that we *ought not* to doubt them. This point is sometimes made by saying that the indubitability of axioms is a psychological, not logical or normative, indubitability. This, I think, is misleading. A man might find it psychologically impossible to think of Abélard without thinking of Héloïse because he is so accustomed to hearing the names linked. This is not the sort of impossibility Descartes has in mind when he speaks of the impossibility of doubting the axioms. If the impossibility he means were a mere psychological impossibility of this kind, it would not be universal, extending even to dreamers. Rather, it is part of the nature of the mind; that is, it is a condition of something's being a mind at all that it should assent to the axioms when they are presented to it.

Are there any propositions at all that are exempt from second-order doubt? What of the *cogito*? Descartes' own existence is called into question afresh in the *Third Meditation*, but in an indirect manner. By analogy with the other texts that list the most evident axioms, it seems clear that the proposition called in question by the second-order doubt is not "I think, therefore I am," but "to think, one must exist," which is said in the *Principles* to give no knowledge of anything existent and therefore cannot be identified with the *cogito* (AT VIII, 8; HR I, 222). But as this axiom is used in the derivation of "*sum*" from "*cogito*," the conclusion "*sum*" is itself called in question. It is not needed for what immediately follows in the *Third Meditation*, since the existence of God is established in the first place not from my existence, but from the existence of the idea of God. The propositions never called into question in Descartes' system are those that report the contents of the mind, those that express the mind's consciousness of its own thoughts and ideas. Thus, the

premise "*cogito*" and the presence of the idea of God
are not challenged by the second-order doubt.

What is the status of the simplest truths of mathematics? Although "2 + 3 = 5" is here presented as if it
had the same first-order indubitability as "What's done
cannot be undone," in the *First Meditation* Descartes
asks, "May not God make me go wrong whenever I add
two and three?"—and this may seem like a first-order
doubt. In the *Seventh Objections,* Bourdin told the
story of a man who while half asleep heard the clock
strike four and said, "The clock is going mad: it has
struck one o'clock four times." Descartes said that this
example "shows that a person adding two and three together can be deceived" (AT VII, 476; HR II, 278).
Once again, the passages are reconcilable if we remember that the impossibility of doubt is not the same thing
as the impossibility of error. Descartes' view appears to
be that if a man has added two and three together, he
cannot be in any doubt about his answer, but his answer may be wrong for all that.

So far, we have been considering truths that can
be intuited. It is time to turn to those that are deduced.
I may see intuitively that a triangle has three sides, but
the theorem that the three angles of a triangle total two
right angles requires a proof that cannot be taken in at
a single mental glance.

> For example the mind has within itself the idea of
> number and figure; it has also among its common
> notations the proposition that "if equals are added
> to equals, the result is equal". From this it is easy
> to demonstrate that the three angles of a triangle

are equal to two right angles. (AT VIII, 9; HR I, 224)

Such a proof leads to clear and distinct perception; and all clear and distinct perception, not just intuition, leads to a certainty that excludes simultaneous doubt (e.g., AT VII, 69; HR I, 183; AT VII, 460; HR II, 266). But conclusions of this kind, unlike the simplest ones shown to us by natural light, can be thought of without being clearly and distinctly perceived. They thus admit of explicit first-order doubt. This may happen in two ways. First, a man may never have discovered a valid proof of a proposition and therefore never have clearly and distinctly perceived it. Second, a man may have produced a proof of a theorem in the past and remembered its conclusion without remembering the steps that led up to it. As long as I attend to the proof of a geometrical theorem, I cannot but believe that it is true.

> But as soon as I turn my mind's eye away from the proof, however much I may remember that I saw it clearly, I may easily come to doubt its truth—supposing I have no knowledge of God. For I can persuade myself that I have been so constituted by nature that I can easily deceive myself in those matters which I believe myself to apprehend with the greatest evidence and certainty. (AT VII, 69; HR I, 184)

It is necessary to stress here that Descartes is not suggesting that he might be inaccurately remembering that he proved something, when in fact he did not. Though he speaks of *"fallax memoria"* Descartes never seriously raises skeptical doubts about the reliability of memory.[3] When Burman objected that even after the proof of the veracious God, a skeptic might say: "Memory deceives me and it seems to me that I recall something which in fact I do not recall," Descartes made no very profound reply. "Of the memory I cannot say anything; every man can tell by experience whether he has a good one; if he is in doubt, he should take notes or use similar aids" (AT V, 148). Descartes' doubt concerns the case in which I do genuinely remember having proved a theorem. Even so, he says, unless convinced of God's veracity I cannot be certain of the theorem.

Descartes has frequently been accused of arguing in a circle in resolving his skeptical doubts by appeal to the veracity of God. Arnauld expressed the circle thus: ". . . we can be sure that God exists, only because we clearly and evidently perceive that he does; therefore prior to being certain that God exists, we should be certain that whatever we clearly and evidently perceive is true." In reply, Descartes distinguished between actual clear and distinct perception and the memory of clear and distinct perception:

> First, we are sure that God exists because we have attended to the proofs that establish this fact; but afterwards it is enough for us to remember that we have perceived something clearly in order to be sure that it is true; but this would not suffice, unless we knew that God existed and that he did not deceive us. (AT VII, 245; HR II, 115)

This reply seems adequate as long as the circle is alleged to have been committed in the justification of those mathematical truths that are open to first-order

doubt. Provided that in the proofs for the existence of
God no appeal is made to remembered perceptions,
there is no circularity in establishing the reliability of remembered perceptions by appeal to the veracity of God,
and Descartes is careful to insist that his proofs of
God's existence do not depend on memory in this way.
In the geometric statement of his system he says that his
readers, by reflecting on the way in which necessary existence is contained in the idea of God, "will learn that
God exists without any train of reasoning" (AT VII,
163; HR II, 55). And when Burman objected that the
Third Meditation proof was long and depended on
many axioms, Descartes denied that this meant that it
could not be seized in a single thought lasting over a
period of time (AT V, 149).[4]

We have seen, however, that the metaphysical
doubt extended not only to mathematical conclusions,
but also to the first-order indubitable axioms used in the
cogito and in the *Third Meditation* proof of God. And
there it does look as if there was circularity in using
these axioms to prove God's existence and in using
God's veracity to resolve the second-order doubt about
them. It seems to have been this circle that Burman
had in mind. The authors of the *Second Objections*
make an analogous point about the proof of *sum res
cogitans.* "You cannot clearly and distinctly know that
you are a thinking thing, since, on your view, that
knowledge depends on clearly knowing the existence of
God, which you have not proved at the point where you
conclude that you know clearly what you are" (AT VII,
125; HR II, 26).

Descartes replied: "When I said that we could

know nothing with certainty unless we know first that
God existed, I said explicitly that I was referring only
to the knowledge of such conclusions as can recur in
memory without our attending further to the reasons
from which we derived them." He was not thinking, he
explained, of the knowledge of first principles or axioms;
and he concluded with the remark, already discussed,
that the *cogito* is not a syllogism (AT VII, 140; HR
II, 38).

In this reply Descartes must be thinking of the
Fifth Meditation, where, having said that without the
knowledge of God it is impossible ever to know anything perfectly, he illustrates by discussing a conclusion
that is recollected without attention to its proof (AT
VII, 70; HR I, 184). But in the *Third Meditation* it is in
connection with intuited axioms that he says, "Without
a knowledge of these two truths (God's existence and
veracity) I do not see that I can ever be certain of anything." It does not seem to the point to insist that in
the *cogito* the principle "in order to think one must
exist" is intuited and not deduced. For it was precisely
intuition that was the subject of second-order doubt.
Thus, it looks as if Descartes was guilty of circularity
in validating intuition, if not in validating deduction.

Harry Frankfurt has argued that we can acquit
Descartes if we regard his procedure as designed to show
not that what is intuited is true, but that there can be
no reasonable grounds for doubting it. Descartes, he
argues, is confronting a skeptic who claims that reason
leads to the conclusion that reason is unreliable. The
skeptic's *reductio ad absurdum* is refuted once it is
shown that the right use of reason leads to the conclu-

sion that there is a veracious deity who guarantees the reliability of reason. For this it is not necessary that the conclusion should be assumed to be true; it is enough that it is shown to be clearly and distinctly perceived. Once this has been done, the skeptic's argument falls and there is no longer reason to doubt the truth of clear and distinct perceptions. The skeptic seeks to show that reason leads to falsehood by showing that it is inconsistent; Descartes can prove that it is consistent without at any point appealing to its truth. So there is no circle as commonly supposed.[5]

In support of his claim that Descartes is comparatively uninterested in the truth of intuition, Frankfurt draws attention to a remarkable passage in the *Second Replies*. If we have a conviction, Descartes says, that is

> . . . so strong that we can never have any cause to doubt that of which we have persuaded ourselves, there is nothing more to inquire about; we have all the certainty that can reasonably be desired. What is it to us, if someone should feign that the very thing of whose truth we are so firmly persuaded appears false to God or to an angel and thus, absolutely speaking, is false? Why should we concern ourselves with this absolute falsity, since we by no means believe in it or even have the least suspicion of it. For we are supposing a conviction so strong that nothing can remove it; and this conviction is in every respect the same as perfect certitude. (AT VII, 145; HR II, 41)

I think that Frankfurt underestimates the extent of Descartes' concern with truth; but he does a service in reminding us what sort of certainty Descartes is looking for. It is not enough, for Cartesian certainty, that I should here and now unhesitatingly make a true judgment on the best possible grounds. It is necessary also that I should be in such a position that I will never hereafter have reason to withdraw that judgment. Whenever I clearly and distinctly perceive something, I cannot help judging that it is so, and this will be a true judgment made on the best possible grounds. But until I have proved the veracity of God, I cannot be sure that I shall not hereafter withdraw this judgment under the influence of the metaphysical suspicion of the omnipotent deceiver. If what I have clearly and distinctly perceived was a demonstrated conclusion, I may later doubt it while explicitly thinking of it. If it was not a conclusion but an axiom, I shall never change my mind about it while it is actually before my mind; but I can doubt it indirectly by doubting whatever seems most evident to me. While the possibility of even this second-order doubt remains, I cannot be said to be certain.

What Descartes seeks, then, is a state of mind that is in a certain sense immutable. This is brought out most clearly in the reply Descartes made to the objection that if his theory of knowledge were true an atheist could not know mathematics.

That an atheist can know clearly that the three angles of a triangle are equal to two right angles I do not deny. I merely affirm that, on the other hand, such knowledge on his part cannot constitute true science, because no knowledge that can be rendered doubtful should be called science. Since he is, as is supposed, an atheist, he cannot be sure that he is not deceived in the things that seem most evident to

him . . . he cannot be safe from this doubt unless
he first recognises the existence of God. (AT VII,
141; HR II, 39)

Mathematical intuition without knowledge of God, he
says in the *Fifth Meditation*, provides "no true and
certain science but only vague and changeable opinions."

The veracity of God, then, is brought in not in
order to prove the truth of what I intuit, but in order to
show that I shall never have reason to change my mind
about what I have once intuited. This is not because
Descartes is uninterested in the truth of the axioms and
conclusions he discusses; on the contrary, his whole
philosophy can be described as "the search after truth."
But there is no better way of establishing the truth of a
proposition than by intuiting it. It is futile to offer a
deductive proof of something that can be better known
by intuition. A *fortiori* it is futile to offer, as a step in
that deductive proof, a demonstration of the existence
and veracity of God.

The appearance of circularity comes about in this
way. Since Descartes offers a proof that whatever is
clearly and distinctly perceived is true, it looks as if he
is trying to establish a major premise for the following
pattern of argument:

Whatever I clearly and distinctly perceive is true.
I clearly and distinctly perceive that *p*.
Therefore, it is true that *p*.

Obviously, there would be circularity in using that
pattern of argument to prove the truth of any proposi-

tion (e.g., that God is veracious) that is necessary in order to establish the major premise. But Descartes is not trying to vindicate such a pattern of argument. When he passes from the clear and distinct perception of something to the affirmation of its truth, he does not do so by tacit appeal to a suppressed major premise; his affirmation is based directly on the intuition and not on a deduction derived from a general proposition about the truthfulness of intuitions. And when, later on, he wonders to himself whether it is really the case that all his intuitions are true, he is not belatedly discovering an unproved assumption in an earlier piece of reasoning, because there was no earlier piece of reasoning. To engage in metaphysical doubt is not to display subtle logical acumen in the detection of implicit premises; it is to betray the weakness of the human intellect that is incapable of holding intuitions steady. It is this human weakness that is to be remedied by the consideration of God's veracity (AT VII, 70; HR I, 174).

That is why Descartes does not offer the veracity of God as a ground for accepting the truth of an intuition. It is not because even the veracity of God will not suffice to show that the intuition may not be, absolutely speaking, false, but because the simple intuition by itself provides both psychologically and logically the best grounds for accepting its truth. Thus, there is no circle. Deduction is called in question, and deduction is vindicated by intuition. The truth of particular intuitions is never called in question, only the universal trustworthiness of intuition, and in vindicating this universal trustworthiness only individual intuitions are utilized. There is no single faculty, or single exercise of a faculty, that is vindicated by its own use. Everything else is vindicated by appeal to "our clearest and most accurate judgements which, if false, cannot be corrected by any that are clearer, or by any other natural faculty" (AT VII, 143; HR II, 40).

Though these judgments cannot themselves be vindicated, Descartes does not think, at the end of his investigations, that they may after all be false in some absolute sense. What then are we to make of the passage from the *Second Replies* quoted by Frankfurt? Decartes does not say that it does not matter if our intuitions appear false to God or to an angel and are therefore absolutely false. He says that it does not matter if someone *feigns* this. Why does it not matter? Because we are certain that what he supposes is only a fiction. "It does not matter if someone imagines that these things appear false to God or an angel, because the evidence of our perception does not permit us to give a hearing to the man who feigns such things" (AT VII, 146; HR II, 42). This does not mean: "Of course, he may be right, but at least we won't listen, and that is the best we can hope for." It means: "Not only is he wrong, but, better than this, we are forearmed against the temptation of listening to him."

The passage occurs in the course of a defense of the thesis that God is no deceiver. If it could be the case that what God makes appear true to us appeared false to Him, then God would most surely be a deceiver. Descartes cannot, therefore, have meant to leave open the possibility that our intuitions are, absolutely speaking, false. The veracity of God suffices to ensure that they are absolutely true. It is not only sufficient, it is also necessary. This is not just because of the transient nature of our intuitions, but also because of the creaturely nature of what we intuit. Since, on Descartes' view, the eternal truths were freely created by God, who might have created them otherwise, nothing can give us certainty about these truths unless, like the natural light in our souls, it is communicated to us by God. Moreover, the only guarantee that we have that "$2 + 2 = 4$" has not changed its truth value since we last intuited it is that God does not change His mind (AT I, 145).

A difficulty arises here. Is not "God cannot deceive" itself an eternal truth? If this too was freely created by God, then He could have made it otherwise. Is there not then a different form of circularity in arguing from the veracity of God to the trustworthiness of our intuitions of the eternal truths? The answer, I think, must be that it was only eternal truths about *creatures* that Descartes thought God was free to make otherwise. To Mersenne he wrote, "He is author of the essence of creatures, as well as of their existence; now this essence is nothing other than the eternal truths" (AT I, 151). In this and similar passages, then, it seems that Descartes was not talking about eternal truths concerning the essence of God. But it is difficult to be sure. Arnauld gave as an example of an eternal truth "God cannot create beings which are independent of him." This appears to be a truth about the nature of God, and Descartes gave no unequivocal reply to Arnauld's question about whether this might cease to be true. But there seems no doubt that he could consistently have answered in the negative.

Descartes' epistemology, then, can be defended

from circularity. Nonetheless, it seems that it is inadequate to achieve its goal. If every other certainty is to be built upon the certainty afforded by clear and distinct perception, then it is essential, if there is to be any certainty at all of the type Descartes sought, that one should be able to be certain that one is clearly and distinctly perceiving something. Moreover, it must be possible to be certain of this independently of being certain of the truth of what one perceives. For Descartes offers it as the sovereign methodological principle for the avoidance of error never to make a judgment about anything that one does not clearly and distinctly understand (AT VII, 61; HR I, 178). If it is to be possible to apply this methodological principle, then it cannot be part of what is meant by "I clearly and distinctly perceive that p" that p is in fact the case. Otherwise, the methodological principle will be as vacuous as the advice "If you want to make money at the races, bet only on horses that are going to win."

Descartes believed that the direct object of the mind's perception was always an idea (*Third Replies*, AT VII, 181; HR II, 68). If we are to achieve knowledge about extramental reality, it can only be by means of true ideas, that is, ideas that conform to their objects (AT II, 597). But how can we tell which ideas are true, since we can have no knowledge of objects independently of ideas? By seeing which ideas are clear and distinct, Descartes always replies. So by another route we reach the same point. If Descartes' method is to be possible at all, then clarity and distinctness must be internal properties of ideas, not properties relating them to extramental objects. And if the method is to lead to the sort of certainty Descartes seeks, it must be impossible to be mistaken about whether one has a clear and distinct idea.[6]

In fact, as Descartes frequently conceded, many people erroneously think that they clearly and distinctly perceive something when they do not do so at all. "There are very few," he said to Bourdin, "who rightly distinguish between that which is really perceived and that which merely seems to be perceived, because few are accustomed to clear and distinct perceptions" (AT VII, 511; HR II, 307). Apart from their truth, there seems to be no criterion by which genuinely clear and distinct perceptions can be distinguished from apparently clear and distinct perceptions. They cannot be distinguished by the degree of conviction that they carry with them; men have died for the sake of ideas that they mistakenly believed to be clear and distinct. They cannot be distinguished by their content, for though there are some topics so simple that no doubt is possible about them, there seem to be none about which no error is possible (AT VII, 476; HR II, 278). They cannot be distinguished for certain by the method of producing them, for though the way to make one's ideas clear and distinct is "to give strenuous attention and study to them, and withdraw one's mind as far as possible from matters corporeal," yet there are some who, even after going through the *Meditations* a thousand times, will fail to clarify their most important ideas (AT III, 430). Time and again Descartes rejects ideas that seem to bear all the internal marks of clarity and distinctness simply on the grounds that he does not consider them true. But if a man cannot tell whether his ideas are genuinely clear and distinct without knowing whether they are true, then he cannot hope to avoid error by using the method of restricting his judgment to what he clearly and distinctly perceives.

NINE

MATTER AND MOTION

One of the things for which Descartes is best remembered is his doctrine that animals are automata. If there were machines, he wrote, with the organs and appearance of a monkey or some other irrational animal, we should have no means of telling that they were not animals (AT VI, 56; HR I, 116). Human beings, he thought, could not be regarded altogether as machines, because of the use of language and because of the universal adaptability of reason. But any human activity that did not depend upon thought was as mechanical as animal activity.

Such are the beating of the heart, the digestion of our food, nutrition, respiration when we are asleep, and even walking, singing, and similar acts when we

are awake, if performed without the mind attending
to them. When a man in falling thrusts out his hand
to save his head he does that without his reason
counselling him so to act, but merely because the
sight of the impending fall penetrating to his brain,
drives the animal spirits into the nerves in the manner
necessary for this motion, and for producing it without the mind's desiring it, and as though it were
the working of a machine. (AT VII, 230; HR II,
104)

This sort of thing, he said:

> . . . will not seem strange to those who know how
> many different automata or moving machines can be
> made by the industry of man, without more than a
> very few parts in comparison with the great multi-
> tude of bones, muscles, nerves, arteries, veins or
> other parts that are found in the body of each animal.
> From this aspect the body is regarded as a machine
> which having been made by the hands of God, is in-
> comparably better arranged, and possesses in itself
> movements which are much more admirable, than
> any of those which can be invented by man. (AT
> VI, 56; HR I, 116)

Among the remarkable properties of the machine of
our body is the circulation of the blood. In describing
the circulation Descartes acknowledged his debt to
Harvey, whose De Motu Cordis had appeared nearly
ten years before the Discourse on Method; though in a
private letter to Mersenne in 1632 he claimed to have
reached his own conclusions before reading Harvey. In
one significant respect, however, Descartes disagreed
with the English doctor. The circulation, he said:

. . . has been so clearly proved by Harvey that it cannot be called in question except by people who are so attached to their prejudices, or so thoroughly disputatious, that they cannot tell true and certain reasons from false and probable ones. But Harvey, it seems to me, has not been so successful in explaining the movement of the heart, because he imagined, against the common opinion of other doctors and the ordinary judgement of sight, that when the heart lengthens, its cavities enlarge, and when it shortens, they become more narrow; on the contrary I claim to demonstrate that they then enlarge. (AT XI, 241)

In fact, Harvey had proved, "against the common opinion of doctors," that it is the contraction, not the dilation of the heart that coincides with the pulse and that the ventricles squeeze the blood they contain into the aorta and pulmonary artery. Descartes maintained, on the contrary, that the blood left the heart in diastole; it was expelled into the arteries because it was rarefied by a "dark fire" in the heart, a fire, he said, similar to that which makes hay hot when shut up before it is dry.

Descartes held resolutely to his incorrect version of the mechanism of circulation. In 1639 he wrote to Mersenne that if what he had written about the movement of the heart should turn out false, then the whole of his philosophy was worthless (AT II, 501).

It was not for experimental reasons that he preferred his own account to Harvey's. True, he began his account by saying: "I should like those not versed in anatomy to take the trouble, before reading this, of having cut up before their eyes the heart of some large animal which has lungs" (AT VI, 47; HR I, 110). But his empirical studies were superficial by comparison with Harvey's[1] and it was on a priori grounds that he commended his theory to those who "know the force of mathematical demonstration" (AT VI, 50; HR I, 112).

He prefers his explanation because it is *mechanistic*. Harvey's account involves treating ventricles as muscular sacs; Descartes' requires nothing but heat, rarefaction, and expansion, properties to be found also in inanimate things. It is because his mechanism stands or falls with the falsity of Harvey's explanation that Descartes says his philosophy is worthless if his account of the heart is mistaken.

Mechanism is the theory that all natural phenomena can be explained by the motion of geometrical matter. It is not just a matter of seeing everything as clockwork; even the simplest clock, as naturally explained, is not a mechanistic system, since it involves the action of *weight*, and weight is neither motion nor a geometrical property of matter. The essence of matter for Descartes, we must recall, is simply extension.

Mechanism is stated most fully in the *Principles*.

I recognize no kind of matter in corporeal objects except that matter susceptible of every sort of division, shape, and motion which geometers call quantity and which they presuppose as the subject matter of their proofs. Further, the only properties I consider in it are those divisions, shapes and motions; and about them I accept only what can be derived from indubitably true axioms with the sort of self-evidence which belongs to a mathematical proof. All natural phenomena, as I shall show, can be explained in this way; I therefore do not think any other principles in physics are either necessary or desirable. (AT VIII, 78)

In his *Replies* to the *Sixth Objections* he says:

I observed that nothing at all belonged to the nature of essence of body except that it was a thing with length and breadth and depth, admitting of various shapes and various motions. I found also that its shapes and motions were only modes, which no power could make to exist apart from it; and on the other hand that colours, odours, savours and the rest of such things, were merely sensations existing in my thought, and differing no less from bodies than pain differs from the shape and motion of the instrument which inflicts it. Finally, I saw that gravity, hardness, the power of heating, of attraction, and of purging, and all other qualities which we experience in bodies, consisted solely in motion or its absence, and in the configuration and situation of their parts. (AT VII, 440; HR II, 254)

In this passage Descartes anticipates Locke's distinction between primary qualities, secondary qualities, and powers.

Descartes draws a number of corollaries from the doctrine that the nature of matter is extension. Since wherever there is extension there is matter, there cannot be a completely empty space or vacuum. Nor can there be any genuine condensation or rarefaction; it is impossible for the same matter to vary in extension. Apparent rarefaction consists in distension by alien matter, as a sponge swells when it absorbs water. How, then, is motion possible if all places are full of body and an identical piece of matter always occupies an equal place? "The only possible movement of bodies is in a circle; a body pushes another out of the place it enters, and this pushes another, and that another till at last we come to a body that enters the place left by the first body at the very moment when the first body leaves it." Motion is defined as "the translation of a piece of matter (a body) from the neighbourhood of the bodies immediately touching it, these being regarded as being at rest, to the neighbourhood of others" (AT VIII, 42–54; HR I, 255–266).

As extension is divisible without limit—it is always possible to conceive of something half as big as anything that has any magnitude at all—so also matter, whose nature is extension, is for Descartes infinitely divisible. Consequently there cannot be any genuine atoms or absolutely indivisible bodies. Nonetheless, Descartes claimed that the world was built up out of tiny bodies of three different sizes, which made the three elements of his system. But these elementary bodies, he insisted, should not be called atoms. Since the heavenly bodies are extended, and since extension is all that is essential to matter, it followed that the sun and the stars are made of the same matter as sublunary bodies, contrary to the opinions of Aristotelian astronomers (AT VIII, 52; HR I, 264).

All natural phenomena are to be explained in terms of matter in motion. God, says Descartes,

> . . . created matter along with motion and rest in the beginning; and now, merely by his ordinary cooperation, he preserves just the quantity of motion and rest in the material world that he put there in

the beginning. Motion, indeed, is only a mode of the moving body; but it has a certain definite quantity, and it is readily conceived that this quantity may be constant in the universe as a whole, while varying in any given part. (AT VIII, 61)

While the total quantity of motion in the universe remains constant, its distribution is settled by the operation of laws of nature. Descartes' first law states that every body, insofar as it is unaffected by extraneous causes, perseveres in the same state of motion or of rest; and the second law that simple or elementary motion is always in a straight line. These laws of inertia he claims to deduce a priori from the immutability of God (AT VIII, 68).

It would take too long, and serve no philosophical purpose, to follow the ingenious theory of vortices, or whirlpools of material particles varying in size and velocity. By means of these vortices Descartes hoped to explain all natural phenomena without appeal either to the Aristotelian notion that bodies have a tendency to travel toward their natural places, or to the hypothesis of a universal gravitation, which had already been put forward by Roberval (AT IV, 401).

Parts of Descartes' system were later confirmed experimentally, and other parts experimentally confuted. But the system is based mainly on a priori philosophical grounds, and it is those grounds that concern us here. Descartes said, "I here present an account of the principal phenomena of nature. Not that we should use these as grounds for proving anything; for our aim is to deduce an account of the effects from the causes, not to deduce an account of the causes from the effects" (AT VIII, 81; HR I, 271).

There are two stages in the a priori account: first, the proof that the essence of matter is extension; then, the proof that no properties but geometrical properties and motion were to be taken into account in giving scientific explanation.

For Descartes the essence of a thing was constituted by those properties that a thing could not cease to have without ceasing to exist. Consequently, his proof that the essence of body is extension consists in a proof that a body may lose any of its properties except its extension, without ceasing to be a body.

> We have only to attend to our idea of some body, e.g. a stone, and remove from it whatever we know is not entailed by the very nature of body. We first reject hardness; for if the stone is melted, or divided into a very fine powder, it will lose this quality without ceasing to be a body. Again, we reject colour; we have often seen stones so transparent as to be colourless. We reject heaviness; fire is extremely light, but none the less conceived as a body. Finally, we reject coldness and heat and all other such qualities; either they are not what we are considering in thinking of the stone, or at least their changing does not mean that the stone is regarded as having lost the nature of a body. We may now observe that absolutely no element of our idea remains, except extension in length, breadth, and depth.

This passage (AT VIII, 65) is reminiscent of a more famous passage about wax in the *Second Meditation*; but there the point is to prove that it is with the intellect, not by the senses, that a human being perceives bodies. The argument seems to be open to objections similar to those Berkeley made against Locke's distinction between primary and secondary qualities. The argument for the permanence of geometric properties seems to depend on taking them generically; a body cannot cease to have some length or other, some breadth or other, some height or other. The argument for the impermanence of some of the other qualities seems to depend on taking them specifically. A body may be weightless or colorless; but must it not have some temperature or other? If one can argue that heat cannot be essential to a body because a body can become cold, can one not argue that length cannot be essential to a body because a body can become short?

This reply, I think, would be unfair. It depends on treating temperature as a scalar magnitude, with heat and cold as vaguely designated points on a single scale. But the view that is at the background of Descartes' argument is that of heat and cold as two opposites, or contraries, by the admixture or temperament of which bodies acquired their felt temperature. It is familiarity with the thermometer, which enables us to measure heat and cold precisely by measuring a geometrical property (the length of a column of mercury), that makes it natural to think of temperature as a scalar magnitude like the geometrical properties with which Descartes here contrasts length. But Descartes is using "heat" in such a way that it is genuinely possible for there to be a body with no heat at all.

Descartes argues that secondary qualities are not only not part of the essence of bodies, they are in a sense not properties of bodies at all. Heat, colors, and tastes are, strictly speaking, mental entities or ideas; and it is a mistake to think "that if a body is hot it has some property just like my idea of heat; that in a white or green object there is the same whiteness or greenness as in my sensation, and in a sweet or bitter body there is the same flavour as I taste" (AT VII, 82; HR I, 193). In fact, we perceive colors only in the sense that we perceive in objects something that produces in us the sensation of color (AT VII, 34; HR I, 296). What we call color, odor, flavor, sound, heat, and cold in external objects is merely the power that these objects have to set our nerves in motion (AT VIII, 323; HR I, 296).

To prove that secondary qualities are mental entities and not real properties of external objects Descartes has four main arguments. The first is that secondary qualities are perceived by one sense only.

> Who has ever doubted that bodies move; that they have various sizes and shapes, and correspondingly varied motions; that the mutual collision of bodies results in the divisions of a bigger body into many smaller ones, and in changes of shape? These facts are observable not just by one sense but by several— by sight, touch, and hearing—moreover, our imagination and conception of them is distinct. The same does not apply to other sensible qualities such as colour and sound; they are not observed by several senses but each by one sense only; and the images of them in our thought are always confused and we are ignorant of their real nature. (AT VIII, 324; HR I, 297)

This seems a poor argument. Why should not properties perceptible by one sense only be objective? It is true that sense impressions of such properties will not be corrigible by the exercise of any other sense; and if a property is to be objective, then it must be possible to correct reports of the occurrence of such properties. But sense impressions of secondary qualities can be corrected in two ways: by further operation of the same sense by the same percipient; and by the cooperation of other observers using the same sense faculty. Reports that an object is red may be shown to be false either by a closer look at the object or by the testimony of other observers. Of course, if colors are just "ideas in the mind," then no correction is possible; a later look just produces a different idea, not further information about the same object, and other people cannot help since they cannot have my ideas. But the thesis that colors are ideas in the mind was supposed to be the conclusion, not the premise, of this argument.

Descartes' second argument is that it is necessary to postulate only primary qualities in things in order to give an adequate physiological account of sensation. As sensation provides the only ground for asserting the existence of secondary qualities, there is, therefore, no reason to accept their objectivity. This less a priori argument will be considered when we discuss Descartes' theory of perception in the next chapter.

The third argument is drawn from the inconceivability of the opposing view. Descartes worked out his position in contrast to the scholastic theory of accidents or real qualities. Colors and tastes and smells were, according to scholastic theory, accidents inhering in substances. Descartes considered the notion of real accidents self-contradictory. "It is inconceivable that real accidents should exist, because whatever can exist separately is not accident but substance" (AT VII, 434;

HR II, 250). He was at one time an adherent of the scholastic view.

> I used to conceive gravity in the fashion of a real quality of a certain order, which inhered in solid bodies; although I called it a quality in so far as it was referred to the bodies in which it inhered, yet because I added the epithet real, I thought in truth it was a substance just as clothing regarded by itself is a substance, although when referred to the man whom it clothes it is quality. (AT VII, 441; HR II, 255)

Further, he argued that if there were real accidents, they would have to be specially created by God in each instance (AT III, 505).

There are many difficulties in the scholastic theory of accidents, but Descartes does not seem to have understood it completely, and the comparison with clothes is misleading. As far as the philosophical theory goes, accidents, qua abstractions, cannot exist without their substances; there cannot be the whiteness of a thing without that of which it is the whiteness. Aquinas wrote:

> Many people make mistakes about forms by judging about them as they would about substances. This seems to come about because forms are spoken of in the abstract as if they were substances, as when we talk of whiteness or virtue or suchlike. So, some people, misled by ordinary usage, regard them as substances. Hence came the error of those who thought that forms must be occult and those who thought that forms must be created . . . A form is described as an entity not because it exists, strictly speaking,

but because something is qualified by means of it
(*aliquid ea est*); thus, too, a form is said to become,
not because it really comes into being, but because
something else, by means of it, comes to be qualified
in a new way (*ea aliquid fit*).[2]

Aquinas' description of the misunderstanding of the
theory of accidental forms fits Descartes very well.
There are indeed special difficulties about the theory
that accidents can remain miraculously without their
subject, as Aquinas believed that in the Eucharist the
whiteness of the bread remained though there was no
longer bread there to be white. But this difficulty arises
not so much from the Aristotelian theory of accidents
as from the Catholic doctrine of transubstantiation; and
that doctrine will give rise to analogous difficulties on
any theory of secondary qualities, including Descartes'
own (cf. AT VII, 248 ff.; HR II, 116). Moreover, the
error of hypostatization—the confusion of the concrete
with the abstract—can arise for primary qualities as
well as for secondary qualities. Both the shape of wax
and its color alike are, on the scholastic theory, accidents.

Descartes' fourth argument, which was the one
that probably most influenced him, was hinted at in the
passage quoted above when he said that the images of
secondary qualities are confused in our thoughts. Secondary qualities do not yield clear and distinct ideas.
"My ideas of cold and heat are so far from being clear
and distinct that I cannot learn from them whether cold
is merely absence of heat, or heat merely absence of
cold; whether both are real qualities or neither is" (AT
VII, 43; HR I, 164). In this context, by "clear and dis-

tinct idea" Descartes cannot mean an idea that resists
Cartesian doubt, for Cartesian doubt is generated by
sense errors involving primary, not secondary, qualities
("Towers which looked round at a distance looked
square when close at hand," etc., AT VII, 76; HR I,
189). Rather, a clear and distinct idea is an idea of the
kind we discussed apropos the ontological argument.
We lack clear and distinct ideas of secondary qualities
in the sense that we cannot make judgments about
them with the certainty of geometry. This was how this
lack was understood by Leibniz, who wrote: "The true
mark of a clear and distinct idea of an object is the
ability one has to know many truths about its object by
a priori proofs."

Why, we may ask, should the only properties that
really belong to things be those that it is possible to
know a priori? This requirement, which seems to us to
be an unscientific prejudice, appeared to Descartes to be
an essential postulate for physics. It is as if he realized
correctly that the way of progress for physics lay through
mathematics, but thought incorrectly that what physics
should imitate in mathematics was not its precise quantification, but its a priori methods of discovery.

It is in fact impossible to show any physical theory
to be true purely on a priori grounds. But of course a
physical theory may be shown a priori to be false if it
can be shown to contain inconsistent elements. Descartes' physical theory seems to be of this kind. I will
mention only two of its internal inconsistencies.

The first instance is that of inertia. Descartes says
that it follows from his first law of nature that everything tends, so far as it can, to remain in the same state

in which it is. Hence, "that which is joined to something else has a certain force to prevent itself being separated from it" (AT VIII, 68). If this force or tendency to move is not a genuine property of a body, but only something in the mind, then it cannot explain physical effects. If it is a genuine property of bodies, then it is untrue that bodies have no properties except geometrical ones plus motion. For a tendency to move cannot be identified with actual motion; the one may be present without the other.

The second instance is that of circular motion. Descartes says that the world is made up of bodies of three different sizes. How are these bodies distinguished? What are the things that have the sizes? For something to have a size, it must have boundaries. What constitutes the boundaries of a single body (or part of matter)? It cannot be any geometrical properties: three-dimensional extension stretches uniformly to infinity. It cannot be any nongeometrical properties other than motion, for there are no such properties. It must, therefore, be a difference in motion between two parts of matter that makes them two. This conclusion Descartes accepts. He says that rest is the strongest glue, and "one body" just means as much of matter as moves together (AT V, 156). Since all motion is in a circle and all the bodies making up the circle move together, they must make one body; thus, the only moving bodies will be complete rotating circles or rings. But motion is the translation of a body from the vicinity of one stationary body to another. But the whole ring, if the bodies within and without it are at rest, does not move. It could move by rotation only if it were possible for one part of the ring to be in contact now with one external body and now with another. But there cannot be distinct parts of the ring unless there are parts of the ring with individual motions of their own. But this is not possible since rings can only move as wholes. Therefore, if Descartes' theory of motion is correct, no motion is possible.

TEN

MIND
AND
BODY

"Although the human soul gives form to the whole body," Descartes wrote in the *Principles*, "its chief seat is in the brain; it is there alone that it performs, not only intellection and imagination, but even sensation" (AT VIII, 315; HR I, 289). Several proofs are offered of this. First, sleep and diseases that affect only the brain interrupt the operation of the senses. Second, if the nerves between external sense organs and the brain are cut, there is no sensation. Third, it is possible to have sensations when the apparent place of the sensation no longer exists. This is the case in the phenomenon of the phantom limb, several times described by Descartes: a girl felt pain in her fingers, though unknown to herself her gangrenous arm had been amputated at the elbow (AT VIII, 320; HR I, 293). Such cases are most naturally explained on the hypothesis that the nerves leading from the affected place to the brain are stimulated in the same manner as they are in the normal case of a genuinely localized pain. Descartes concludes that "the soul feels those things that affect the body not in so far as it is in each member of the body, but only in so far as it is in the brain" (ibid.). But his arguments seem to establish only that the brain is necessary for sensation, not that it is sufficient by itself. They do not show, for instance, that the nerves are not also necessary.

However, Descartes is more anxious to show that it is possible that mere motions of the animal spirits, or tiny fluids, in the nerves can be capable of causing such varied sensations as those of heat and cold and color and light. He points out that a bang on the head may cause one to see stars, stopping up one's ear causes murmuring, cutting with a knife may cause pain; in all these cases we have sensation produced by mere motion. Moreover, he draws a number of analogies. Letters written with the few characters of the alphabet can convey to us information about the most diverse scenes and produce a rich variety of emotions. A blind man, feeling his way with two sticks, may find out much about the shape and position of objects that we find out with our eyes. Moreover, in the nerves themselves that lead from the organs to the brain, we detect nothing but motion. Hence, Descartes concludes:

. . . we must on all counts conclude that the objective external realities that we designate by the words *light, colour, odour, flavour, sound,* or by names of tactile qualities such as *heat* and *cold*, are not recognizably other than the powers that objects have to set our nerves in motion in various ways, according to their own varied disposition. (AT VII, 323; HR I, 296)

"It is the soul that sees," said Descartes, "and not the eye; and only by means of the brain does the immediate act of seeing take place" (AT VI, 113). He said this on the grounds that *what* a man sees is causally determined ultimately by the condition of his brain at the moment of seeing; and he appealed especially to brain disorders to establish his point. "This is why maniacs and men asleep often see, or think they see, objects that are not before their eyes; certain vapours disturb the brain, and produce the same disposition of the region normally employed for sight as though the objects were present."

Descartes arrived at his position by taking seriously optical illusions and errors of sense. Consider the familiar case of the straight stick that looks bent when half-immersed in water. In such a case, Descartes believed, three things happened: (1) light rays reflected from the stick excited motions in the animal spirits in the optic nerve and thus affected the brain, (2) an idea of color and light results in the mind, and (3) the will makes a judgment that the stick is bent. It is the second that is really called sensation; the first could occur purely mechanically in animals, and the third does not occur when the cautious man refrains from misjudging the stick. The result of this threefold apparatus is that in what is strictly called sensation—the idea in the mind—there is no error. There can be mistaken judgment and there can be mechanical breakdown, but the pure sensation cannot be mistaken, and so the interests of epistemology and theodicy are safeguarded.

It is interesting to compare Descartes' account of error with that of Aquinas, who treats it in his question *whether there is falsehood in sensation.*[1] Like Descartes, Aquinas says that neither truth nor falsehood directly belongs to sense, but only to intellectual judgment; nonetheless, the sense makes a kind of judgment, taking a thing to be of a certain kind, and this may be mistaken —*per accidens*—and because of the indisposition of the organ. Unlike Descartes, Aquinas thinks that there is a likeness of the thing sensed in the sense: there is a likeness of color in sight and flavor in taste. Strictly speaking, he says, it is not the eye that sees, or the soul, but the whole animal.

What is at issue in the question "Are secondary qualities in objects *like* sensations?" If the question asks what things really look like when nobody is looking at them, then it is obviously foolish. Aquinas was not committed to the theory that things actually tasted sweet when no one was tasting them; the Aristotelian explanation was that things untasted were sweet only potentially, and tasting sweet in this sense was precisely to have the power to taste sweet to a tasting animal.

What, then, differentiates the Aristotelian view from Descartes' view that secondary qualities are "powers that objects have"? For Descartes the power was to set our nerves in motion; for Aquinas it was to produce likenesses of themselves. And this difference in turn comes down to this: Aquinas thought it correct, while Descartes thought it incorrect, to predicate the felt qualities of the objects themselves. In this, it seems to me, Aquinas is more correct than Descartes. Descartes thought redness could not be in the object because it could be produced in the mind by other causes and because even when it was apparently in the object it could fail to reach the mind owing to interruptions in the nervous system. But let us apply Descartes' own analogy of letters; let us treat the information that reaches us from the external world as if it were a set of messages delivered by a postal service. The fact that a letter written from a battlefield may be intercepted or that letters can be forged purporting to be from battlefields does not show at all that no letters can ever come from battlefields, still less that no letters are ever really *about* battlefields. But Descartes is much clearer than Aquinas that the means by which information reaches us about the properties of external objects need not itself possess the properties of which it informs us.

Aquinas seems to be correct against Descartes on the fundamental point that what senses is not the organ or the soul, but the whole animal. To discover whether an unknown animal has vision or not we have to study the behavior of his whole body to ascertain whether he can discriminate between colors or between light and darkness. Once again, Descartes can be corrected by an appeal to one of his own metaphors. He frequently compares the human body to a clock. A human being making a sense error is compared in the *Sixth Meditation* to a clock telling the wrong time (AT VII, 85; HR I, 195). To tell the wrong time is something that only a whole clock can do. The cause of the error may be in

a particular part of the clock—say, the escapement—
but the escapement does not tell the wrong time, only
the clock of which the faulty escapement is a part.
Similarly, though a sense error may be due to an indisposition in a particular part of the body, it is the whole
animal that makes the mistake. It is not that the soul
sees what is presented to it by the malfunctioning body;
it is rather that the whole animal fails to see what is
presented to it, because of a disorder in a part of it.

From a philosophical point of view this account
of error can be summed up in Aquinas' statement that
error is *per accidens* and *propter indispositionem organi*.
But if Descartes' theory is philosophically less subtle, it
is physiologically very much more fertile. First, he had
the curiosity and skill Aquinas lacked to investigate the
precise nature of the indisposition of the organ. Second,
he constructed a theoretical mechanical model of perception, which could suggest testable physiological
hypotheses. Third, his concern to reconcile the good-
ness of the author of nature with the possibility of sense
deception gave him an insight into the survival value of
the mechanisms of perception and the natural sensations of hunger, thirst, and pain (AT VII, 84 ff.; HR
I, 194 ff.).

In all these ways Descartes improved upon his
scholastic predecessors, so that he was justified in com-
plaining to Voetius of the barrenness and impracticality
of scholastic philosophy. It may be philosophically ir-
reproachable to say that opium puts one to sleep because of its dormitive power; but it is scientifically un-
helpful. We want to know how it does this and in what
ingredient its power resides. By observation, experiment,

and mathematical analysis Descartes was able to make considerable advances in optics, offering explanations of the estimation of distance and the phenomena of visual size constancy that still impress specialists in the field.[2]

These advances in physiology, ironically, were not allowed by Descartes' own principles to be reckoned as accounts of perception in the strictest sense. The physiological processes were not parts of perception, only preambles to the purely mental event that alone fully deserved to be called "sensation." The link between the mechanistic events in the body and the spiritual events in the soul was something Descartes was never able to explain satisfactorily.

In the *Sixth Meditation* Descartes insisted, "I am not lodged in my body only as a pilot in a vessel, I am very closely united with it so that I seem to compose with it one whole." If that were not so, he argued, "when my body is hurt, I, who am merely a thinking thing, should not feel pain, for I should perceive this wound by the understanding only, just as a sailor perceives by sight when something is damaged in his vessel." Hunger, thirst and pain, he went on, are confused modes of thought produced by the union and apparent intermingling of mind and body. God could have linked these thoughts with different processes in body and brain; but in no other way could He have provided as well as He has done for the conservation of the body (AT VII, 81, 88; HR I, 192, 197).

These remarks make clear *that* soul and body are connected and *why* they should be connected as they are; but they do not explain *how* they are connected. On Descartes' principles it is difficult to see how an unextended thinking substance can cause motion in an extended unthinking substance and how the extended unthinking substance can cause sensations in the unextended thinking substance. The properties of the two kinds of substance seem to place them in such diverse categories that it is impossible for them to interact. Yet Descartes constantly uses causal language for the relationship between the two.

In attacking the scholastic doctrine of real qualities, Descartes wrote in the *Principles*:

> We can very well conceive how the movement of one body can be caused by that of another, and diversified by the size, figure, and situation of its parts, but we can in nowise understand how these same things (viz. size, figure and motion) can produce something entirely different in nature from themselves, such as are those substantial forms and real qualities which many suppose to exist in bodies; nor likewise can we understand how these forms or qualities possess the force adequate to cause motion in other bodies. (AT VIII, 322; HR I, 295)

Substitute "thoughts" for "forms and qualities" in this passage, and you have a criticism that struck many contemporaries as applicable to Cartesianism itself.

Princess Elizabeth asked Descartes how mind and body could interact. In reply he distinguished between four sorts of primitive notions within us: those that apply to everything conceivable, as *being, number, duration*; those that apply to body alone, as *extension*; those that apply to soul alone, as *thought*; and those that apply to body and soul, as their *union* with each other. After this promising preamble, he had only two things to say: first, that the action of soul on body was rather like that which the scholastics mistakenly attributed to gravity; second, that the union of soul and body was perceived better by sense than by intellect, and therefore it was best not to philosophize too much about it. But of course Elizabeth's question was not *whether* body and soul were united, but *how*; and the inconceivability of this is not lessened by being compared to another inconceivable (AT III, 665).

Elizabeth wrote that it was more easy to attribute matter and extension to the soul than it was to attribute to an immaterial soul the capacity to move and be moved by bodies. Descartes told her to feel free to do so, since to attribute matter and extension to the soul was simply to conceive it as united to the body. But this answer was hardly fair. Extension as defined by Descartes could not be a genuine attribute of soul as defined by Descartes; the one is divisible and the other indivisible. Moreover, as he added in the same letter, the extension of matter determines it to a certain place from which it excludes all other bodily extension; while the extension of thought does not do so at all (AT III, 677).

Descartes' fullest account of the relationship between soul and body comes in *The Passions of the Soul*, which was in part the fruit of his correspondence with Elizabeth. In this we are told that "although the soul is joined to the whole body, there is yet in that a certain part in which it exercises its function more particularly than in all the others." This, we learn, is neither the heart, nor the whole brain, but the pineal gland, "the most inward of all the parts of the brain," and the only organ in it that is single and not divided into right and left parts. The pineal gland is suspended in the center of the brain in contact with the animal spirits reaching the brain through pipelike nerves in such a way that it can move the muscles and be moved by sensory stimuli in accordance with the flow of animal spirits in an inward or outward direction.

> Thus, for example, if we see some animal approach us, the light reflected from its body depicts two images of it, one in each of our eyes, and these two images form two others, by means of the optic nerves, in the interior surface of the brain which faces its cavities; then from there, by means of the animal spirits with which its cavities are filled, these images so radiate towards the little gland which is surrounded by these spirits, that the movement which forms each point of one of the images tends towards the same point of the gland towards which tends the movement which forms the point of the other image, which represents the same part of this animal. By this means the two images which are in the brain form but one upon the gland, which, acting immediately upon the soul, causes it to see the form of this animal. (AT XI, 19; HR I, 345-347)

In this passage we see Descartes exercising physiological ingenuity in an unsuccessful attempt to solve a fundamentally philosophical problem. If interaction between thought and matter is inconceivable, then interaction between soul and gland presents no less a problem than interaction between soul and body. Moreover, Descartes' theory that the real agent in seeing is not the man but the soul leads to the theory that the real object of sight is not anything outside the body but patterns on the pineal gland. In the *Dioptrics* he warned against thinking that there are eyes behind our eyes with which we study the images on the retina. But to use the language of perception for the relation between soul and gland is to speak in terms that would only be appropriate if the soul were a homunculus with miniature eyes.

Descartes had once hoped to further the science of medicine by his studies of metaphysics and physics. As he grew older, he became more and more troubled by the difficulties concerning the relationship between mind and body. When Gassendi asked, "What must the union of the corporeal with the incorporeal be?" he replied, "at no place do you bring an objection to my arguments." But later, when Elizabeth asked how a thinking soul could move the animal spirits, he answered, "I may truly say that what your Highness proposes seems to me to be the question people have most right to ask me in view of my published works" (AT III, 663). Toward the end of his life he wrote to Chanut that though he had spent more time on medicine than ethics, his ethical studies were succeeding better than his medical ones. He concluded with sad resignation: "Instead of finding the means to preserve my life, I have found another way, far easier and far safer, which is not to be afraid of death." [3]

NOTES

Chapter Two

1. J. L. Austin, *Sense and Sensibilia* (London: Oxford University Press, 1962), p. 48.
2. Norman Malcolm, *Dreaming* (London: Routledge, 1959), p. 109.
3. Henri Gouhier, *Essais sur Descartes* (Paris: Vrin, 1937), p. 163 (translation mine).
4. O. K. Bouwsma, "Descartes' Evil Genius," *The Philosophical Review*, LVIII (Jan., 1949), 150.
5. Thomas Aquinas, *Summa Theologiae*, Ia, 25, 3.
6. See E. Brehier, "La Création des vérités éternelles dans la système de Descartes," *Descartes* (Paris: Alcan, 1937), pp. 15–29.

Chapter Three

1. Jacques Chevalier, *Descartes* (Paris: Plon, 1921), p. 218.

2. A. J. Ayer, *The Problem of Knowledge* (Harmondsworth: Penguin, 1956), p. 46.

3. Jaakko Hintikka, "*Cogito, Ergo Sum*: Inference or Performance," *The Philosophical Review*, LXXI (Jan., 1962), 3–32.

4. *Ibid.*, p. 18n.

5. Hintikka's article was criticized by Julius R. Weinberg, "Some Reflections on Mr. Hintikka's Article," *The Philosophical Review*, LXXI (Oct., 1962), 483–491; by James D. Carney, "*Cogito Ergo Sum* and *Sum Res Cogitans*," *The Philosophical Review*, LXXI (Oct., 1962), 492; and by Harry G. Frankfurt, "Descartes' Discussion of His Existence in the Second Meditation," *The Philosophical Review*, LXXVI (July, 1966), 329–358.

6. A. N. Prior, "The *Cogito* of Descartes and the Concept of Self-Confirmation," *The Foundation of Statements and Decisions* (Berlin: Suhrkamp, 1965).

7. See Weinberg, *op. cit.*, and Hintikka, "*Cogito Ergo Sum* as an Inference and a Performance," *The Philosophical Review*, LXXII (Oct., 1963), 487–496.

8. This is pointed out by Frankfurt, *op. cit.*

9. I am indebted for the realization of this to Frankfurt's article, *ibid.*

10. Bertrand Russell, *History of Western Philosophy* (London: Allen and Unwin, 1961), p. 550.

11. Peter Geach, *Mental Acts* (London: Routledge, n.d.), pp. 117–121.

Chapter Four

1. The importance of this text is pointed out by L. J. Beck, *The Metaphysics of Descartes* (London: Oxford University Press, 1965), p. 117. Unfortunately, Beck mistranslates the passage.

2. See the Translator's Note in Elizabeth Anscombe and Peter Thomas Geach, *Descartes: Philosophical Writings* (London: Nelson, 1954), p. xlvii.

3. See the controversy between M. Gueroult and F. Alquié in *Descartes, Cahiers de Royaumont* (Paris: Editions de Minuit, 1957), p. 180.

4. Gilbert Ryle, *The Concept of Mind* (London: Hutchinson, 1949), p. 130.

5. The Latin version of Descartes' replies to Hobbes tells us that cogitative acts *"omnes sub ratione communi cogitationis, sive perceptionis, sive conscientiae conveniunt."* The French version has *"tous lesquels conviennent entre eux en ce qu'ils ne peuvent être sans pensée, ou perception, ou conscience et connaissance."*

6. L. Wittgenstein, *Philosophical Investigations* (Oxford: Blackwell, 1953), I, 243 ff. I have developed the argument at greater length in my paper "Cartesian Privacy," in *Wittgenstein,* G. Pitcher (ed.) (New York: Doubleday, 1966), pp. 252–370.

7. See A. N. Prior, *Formal Logic* (London: Oxford University Press, 1955), p. 189.

8. Norman Malcolm, "Descartes' Proof that His Essence Is Thinking," *The Philosophical Review,* LXXIV (July, 1965), 315–338. Although I disagree with the conclusions of this article, I am indebted to it for several illuminating suggestions.

9. *Ibid.,* p. 319.

Chapter Five

1. See L. J. Beck, *The Metaphysics of Descartes* (London: Oxford University Press, 1965), p. 152.

2. Aristotle, *De Anima* III, 429b 6–10.

3. In the *Rules* cerebral images are called "ideas" (AT X, 443; HR I, 56).

Chapter Six

1. See E. Gilson, *René Descartes: Discours de la méthode, texte et commentaire* (Paris: Vrin, 1962), p. 324.

2. Elizabeth Anscombe and Peter Thomas Geach, *Descartes: Philosophical Writings* (London: Nelson, 1954), p. 81.

3. G. Frege, *Philosophical Writings*, Geach and Black (eds.) (Oxford: Blackwell, 1952), p. 125.

4. Peter Thomas Geach, "The Law of Excluded Middle," *Supplementary Proceedings of the Aristotelian Society*, XXX (1956), 65.

5. Hume, *Treatise of Human Nature*, I, III, iii.

6. A. N. Prior, "On the Unity of Professor Carnap," *Mind*, LXXIII (Oct., 1966), 268.

7. John Passmore, *Philosophical Reasoning* (London: Duckworth, 1961), pp. 28–30.

Chapter Seven

1. E. Gilson, *René Descartes: Discours de la méthode, texte et commentaire* (Paris: Vrin, 1962), p. 347.

2. I have defended this interpretation more fully in

my paper "Descartes' Ontological Argument," in *Fact and Existence*, J. Margolis (ed.) (Oxford: Blackwell, 1968),

3. Alexius Meinong, "The Theory of Objects," translated in *Realism and the Background of Phenomenology*, R. Chisholm (ed.) (Glencoe, Ill.: Free Press, 1960), pp. 76 ff. The passages quoted are from pp. 82, 83, 86, respectively.

4. Hume, *Treatise of Human Nature*, I, III, 7.

5. The argument, however, was accepted by Russell, who reproduced it in *The Philosophy of Leibniz* (London: Allen and Unwin, 1903), p. 174.

6. See C. J. F. Williams, "Aristotle and Corruptibility," *Religious Studies*, I (1966), 97, who cites Aquinas, In Lib. I, *de Caelo et Mundo*, lectio xxvi, no. 6.

7. Norman Malcolm, "Anselm's Ontological Argument," *The Philosophical Review*, LXIX (Jan., 1960), 48.

8. B. Russell, review of Meinong's *Untersuchungen zur Gegenstandstheorie*, *Mind*, XIV (Oct., 1905), 532ff. I am indebted for this reference to R. Chisholm.

9. W. V. O. Quine, "On What There Is," in *From a Logical Point of View* (Cambridge, Mass.: Harvard University Press, 1961).

Chapter Eight

1. See Thomas Aquinas, *Summa Theologiae*, Ia, 58, 3.

2. See Harry G. Frankfurt, "Descartes' Validation of Reason," *American Philosophical Quarterly*, 2 (April, 1965), 149–156; an article to which I am greatly indebted.

3. See Willis Doney, "The Cartesian Circle," *Journal of the History of Ideas*, 16 (Oct., 1955), 324–338, and Harry G. Frankfurt, "Memory and the Cartesian Circle," *The Philosophical Review*, LXXI (Oct., 1962), 504–511.

4. Since both proofs can be intuited, I do not see

that it makes any difference, from the point of view of circularity, whether the ontological argument is placed first (as in the *Principles*) or placed second (as in the *Meditations*), *pace* M. Gueroult, *Nouvelles reflexions sur la preuve ontologique des Descartes* (Paris: Vrin, 1955).

5. Frankfurt, "Descartes' Validation of Reason," *op. cit.*

6. See the excellent articles by Alan Gewirth, "The Cartesian Circle," *The Philosophical Review*, L (Oct., 1941), 309 ff., and "Clearness and Distinctness in Descartes," *Philosophy*, 18 (Jan., 1942), 11 ff.

Chapter Nine

1. See L. Chauvois, *Descartes, sa methode et ses erreurs en physiologie* (Paris: Cedre, 1966).

2. For this quotation, and for many of the ideas contained in this chapter, I am indebted to Peter Hoenen, *Cosmologia* (Rome: P. U. G., 1949), pp. 136 ff. The quotation from Aquinas is *Q. D. De Virt. in comm.*, 11.

Chapter Ten

1. Thomas Aquinas, *Summa Theologiae*, Ia, 17, 3.

2. See R. L. Gregory, *Eye and Brain* (London: Weidenfeld & Nicholson, 1966), pp. 152–153.

3. These passages are cited by Etienne Gilson, *The Unity of Philosophical Experience* (New York: Scribner, 1937), p. 198.

FOR
FURTHER
READING

There is an admirable complete bibliography of the Cartesian literature, with entertaining critical comments, in Gregor Sebba's *Bibliographia Cartesiana 1800–1960* (The Hague: Nijhoff, 1964). Below I list a selection of works in English.

TRANSLATIONS

Philosophical Works of Descartes, Elizabeth S. Haldane and G. R. T. Ross, translators (Cambridge: Cambridge University Press, 1967), 2 volumes, paperback. The most complete collection in English of Descartes' writings.

Descartes: Philosophical Writings, Elizabeth Anscombe and Peter Thomas Geach, editors and translators (London: Thomas Nelson & Sons, 1954). A more vigorous and philosophically more sophisticated translation, less complete and occasionally more controversial than the above.

Descartes: Philosophical Writings, Norman Kemp Smith, editor and translator (New York: Modern Library, 1958).

BOOKS

Balz, A. G. A., *Descartes and the Modern Mind* (New Haven and London: Yale University Press and Oxford University Press, 1952).

Beck, L., *The Method of Descartes* (London: Oxford University Press, 1952).

——, *The Metaphysics of Descartes* (London: Oxford University Press, 1965).

Haldane, E. S., *Descartes, His Life and Times* (London: Murray, 1905).

Keeling, S. V., *Descartes* (London: Benn, 1934).

Maritain, J., *The Dream of Descartes* (London: Editions Poetry, 1945).

Nakhnikian, G., *An Introduction to Philosophy* (New York: Knopf, 1967).

Plantinga, A., *The Ontological Argument* (New York: Doubleday, 1965).

Roth, L., *Descartes' Discourse on Method* (Oxford: Clarendon Press, 1937).

Ryle, G., *The Concept of Mind* (London: Hutchinson, 1949).

Smith, N. Kemp, *New Studies in the Philosophy of Descartes* (London: Macmillan, 1952).

ARTICLES

A number of papers concerned with Descartes' *Meditations* have been usefully collected in a paperback entitled

Meta-meditations, Alexander Sesonske and Noel Fleming, editors (Belmont: Wadsworth, 1966). In addition to this collection, the following papers may be mentioned.

Ayer, A. J., *The Problem of Knowledge* (Harmondsworth: Pelican, 1956), Chap. 2.

Doney, W., "The Cartesian Circle," *Journal of the History of Ideas*, XVI (Oct., 1955), 324–338.

Frankfurt, H. G., "Memory and the Cartesian Circle," *Philosophical Review*, LXXI (Oct., 1962).

———, "Descartes' Validation of Reason," *American Philosophical Quarterly*, 2 (April, 1965).

———, "Descartes' Discussion of His Existence in the Second Meditation," *Philosophical Review*, LXXVI (July, 1966).

Gewirth, A., "The Cartesian Circle," *Philosophical Review*, L (Oct., 1941).

———, "Clearness and Distinctness in Descartes," *Philosophy*, 18 (Jan., 1942).

Williams, B. A. O., "Descartes," in *The Concise Encyclopedia of Western Philosophy and Philosophers*, J. D. Urmson, editor (London: Hutchinson, 1960).

———, "Descartes," in *The Encyclopedia of Philosophy*, Paul Edwards, editor (New York: Macmillan, 1967).

Some of these and other valuable papers are now available in Willis Doney's *Descartes: A Collection of Critical Essays* (New York: Doubleday, 1967).

INDEX

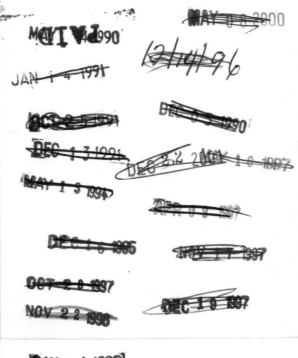